UNDERSTANDING
RANDALL JARRELL

Understanding Contemporary American Literature

Matthew J. Bruccoli, *Editor*

Understanding Bernard Malamud
   by Jeffrey Helterman
Understanding James Dickey
   by Ronald Baughman
Understanding John Hawkes
   by Donald J. Greiner
Understanding Thomas Pynchon
   by Robert D. Newman
Understanding Randall Jarrell
   by J. A. Bryant, Jr.

UNDERSTANDING
Randall
JARRELL

BY J. A. BRYANT, JR.

UNIVERSITY OF SOUTH CAROLINA PRESS

Copyright © University of South Carolina 1986

Published in Columbia, South Carolina, by the
University of South Carolina Press

Manufactured in the United States of America

Library of Congress Cataloging-in-Publication Data

Bryant, J. A. (Joseph Allen), 1919–
    Understanding Randall Jarrell.

    (Understanding contemporary American literature)
    Bibliography: p.
    Includes index.
    1. Jarrell, Randall, 1914–1965—Criticism and
interpretation.   I. Title.   II. Series.
PS3519.A86Z595   1986   811'.52   86-11300
ISBN 0-87249-487-X
ISBN 0-87249-488-8 (pbk.)

CONTENTS

EDITOR'S PREFACE

Understanding Contemporary American Literature has been planned as a series of guides or companions for students as well as good nonacademic readers. The editor and publisher perceive a need for these volumes because much of the influential contemporary literature makes special demands. Uninitiated readers encounter difficulty in approaching works that depart from the traditional forms and techniques of prose and poetry. Literature relies on conventions, but the conventions keep evolving; new writers form their own conventions—which in time may become familiar. Put simply, *UCAL* provides instruction in how to read certain contemporary writers—identifying and explicating their material, themes, use of language, point of view, structures, symbolism, and responses to experience.

The word *understanding* in the series title was deliberately chosen. Many willing readers lack an adequate understanding of how contemporary literature works; that is, what the author is attempting to express and the means by which it is conveyed. Although the criticism and analysis in the series have been aimed at a level of general accessibility, these introductory volumes are meant to be applied in con-

EDITOR'S PREFACE

junction with the works they cover. Thus they do not provide a substitute for the works and authors they introduce, but rather prepare the reader for more profitable literary experiences.

M. J. B.

UNDERSTANDING
RANDALL JARRELL

CHAPTER ONE

Understanding Randall Jarrell

Career

Randall Jarrell was born on May 6, 1914, in Nashville, Tennessee. While still an infant, he was taken by his parents to Long Beach, California. When his parents separated in 1925, Jarrell remained there for a year, living with his great-grandmother and paternal grandparents. Back with his mother in Nashville, he completed public school and entered Vanderbilt University, where he majored in psychology but came under the influence of the Fugitive poets, notably John Crowe Ransom. Subsequently as a graduate student in English he began writing a thesis on W. H. Auden under Ransom's direction.

In 1937 Jarrell followed Ransom to Kenyon College, where he taught the freshman survey, coached the tennis team, and roomed with Robert Lowell. Peter Taylor joined them there the following year. In 1939 Jarrell completed his M.A. thesis at Vanderbilt (now on A. E. Housman) under the direction of Donald Davidson and moved to the University of Texas,

where he taught English for the next three years. There
he met and married Mackie Langham and published
twenty of his poems in a New Directions volume entitled *Five Young American Poets*.

During the war years, which he spent at army air-
fields in Texas, Illinois, and Arizona, Jarrell published
two volumes of poetry: *Blood for a Stranger* (1942)
and *Little Friend, Little Friend* (1945). Afterward he
served as literary editor for *The Nation* for a year and
taught part-time at Sarah Lawrence College. In 1947
both Jarrells joined the faculty of the Women's College
of the University of North Carolina at Greensboro,
and during the next six years Randall published two
volumes of poetry, *Losses* (1948) and *The Seven-
League Crutches* (1951); continued to write critical essays; produced a novel, *Pictures from an Institution*
(1954); and accepted visiting appointments at Colorado,
Princeton, Indiana, and Illinois. He and his wife separated in 1951 and were divorced in 1952, but Jarrell remained at Greensboro. In November of 1952 he married
Mary von Schrader.

Between 1952 and 1962 Jarrell produced, in addition to *Pictures from an Institution*, two collections of
criticism, *Poetry and the Age* (1953) and *A Sad Heart
at the Supermarket* (1962), a volume of *Selected
Poems* (1955), and a new book of poetry, *The Woman
at the Washington Zoo* (1960), which won a National
Book Award. He also edited Kipling's short fiction,

produced an anthology of Russian short novels, served as judge for the Bollingen and the National Book Awards, and spent two years (1956–58) as poetry consultant at the Library of Congress. In 1963 he made a trip to Europe (his third), working steadily meanwhile on a version of *Faust*, and in 1964–65 published his three books for children, *The Gingerbread Rabbit*, *The Bat-Poet*, and *The Animal Family*. Jarrell's last volume of poems, *The Lost World*, appeared in 1965, the year of his accidental death on a road near Chapel Hill, North Carolina.

Complete Poems and *The Third Book of Criticism* came out in 1969; *Fly by Night*, another children's book in 1976; *Kipling, Auden & Co.*, a collection of unpublished reviews and essays, in 1980; and the letters, edited by Mary Jarrell, in 1985.

Overview

Early in 1942, having put together his first volume of poetry, *Blood for a Stranger*, Randall Jarrell wrote an essay for *The Nation* entitled "The End of the Line."[1] In it, with characteristic confidence, he listed thirteen distinctive features of modernist poetry and then proceeded to declare the resulting complex of qualities he had set down as "essentially romantic." At the beginning of the essay he had defined romanticism as a "constant experimentalism, the indefinite attainment of 'originality' "; and he also made experimentalism the first criterion for his modernism. Other features that he listed were an external formlessness, emotional intensity, obscurity, a lack of restraint, a preoccupation with sensations and with dreams, irony, the use of neoprimitive elements, individualism, isolation, alienation, and a hostility to the "progressive" developments of modern western culture.[2]

Jarrell's ostensible point in the essay was that romanticism in its contemporary guise of modernism had at last come to a dead end. Privately he was probably more concerned to cast disapproving glances at a few poets who in his view had reached the limit of their capability; but in any case, he had given a good description of what was to be his own practice as a poet. Thus it is understandable that although he went on to publish two volumes of criticism and plan a third, he never saw fit to reprint "The End of the Line" with its sweeping, dispiriting, and premature conclusion that what he had called modernism was dead. Romantic modernism as he had characterized it would continue throughout the rest of his career to provide both the mode for his own poetry and the context for his criticism of the poetry of others.

Some of the characteristics of Jarrell's modernism may have been the result of imitation—for example, the witty criticism of society that in the beginning was strongly reminiscent of Auden—but other character-istics were simply a part of his nature. One of these was that individualism (with its natural concomitants, isolation and alienation) which characterized almost everything he did. Some might suggest that the inten-sity and the persistence of his posture in this regard re-flected the personalist, or panpsychist, bias of the Vanderbilt philosopher Herbert C. Sanborn, under whom he had studied and whom he came to know closely during Sanborn's association with the Vander-bilt Fugitive-Agrarians, John Crowe Ransom, Donald Davidson, Allen Tate, and Robert Penn Warren. But Jarrell's natural inclination to go his own way was dis-cernible to acquaintances long before his Vanderbilt days, and one suspects that he himself grasped the ne-cessity for accepting and making the most of it as soon as he began to recognize that he possessed certain en-dowments of genius which, for the most part, the rest of the world lacked. If the reports of old friends can be believed, early in life Jarrell was already manifesting the extraordinary confidence in the validity of his own taste that characterizes the first essays and reviews of his adulthood. To be sure, his rational capabilities were more than sufficient to have uncovered the basis for any preference he chose to enunciate, but he was usually reluctant to deploy them to that end. For him

UNDERSTANDING RANDALL JARRELL

it was quite enough to know that he liked something or disliked it and to say so firmly and, if possible, unforgettably. He assumed that the reasons for his judgment would be self-evident.

Moreover, since taste was Jarrell's primary arbiter, his preferences tended to assume the emotional intensity of passions. Thus in the name of taste he could be zealous in his advocacy of Rilke, Proust, Mahler, or Renaissance painting and by the same token contemptuous of poems, musical compositions, or paintings that he disliked. It is not surprising, therefore, that his judgments were sometimes disturbing to those who happened to be in disagreement, especially when those judgments were delivered with a wit that was condescending at best and sometimes devastating. To Jarrell's credit, however, his judgments were also the product of an honesty which in time he applied as uncompromisingly to himself as to other persons and things; and, though at first some misunderstood, most people eventually came to recognize that his lash was matched by a fund of sympathy which instinctively he extended to all kinds and conditions of people, including people he had wounded. As Jarrell grew older and learned to temper his wit, his capacity for sympathy became a conspicuous aspect of his personality; but that aspect had been quietly dominant all along, and nowhere more evident than in his poetry.

UNDERSTANDING RANDALL JARRELL

One sees an obvious manifestation of it in his fondness for the dramatic monologue, which for Jarrell, as for Rilke before him, served as one means of identifying with a broad range of human experience.[3] Among the most memorable examples are those poems in which he speaks with the voice of a woman—for example, his version of Hugo von Hofmannsthal's aging Marschallin in *Der Rosenkavalier*, who in Jarrell's "The Face" becomes, as Ransom noted, the tragic figure of Everywoman in the twenty-six short lines that Jarrell gives her.[4] The woman's voice is noteworthy also in the aging modern housewife in "Next Day"; the widow of the dead airman in "Burning the Letters"; the deranged wife of a well-meaning but insensitive husband in "Seele im Raum"; and the mother of two children, one dead and one grown and independent, in "The Lost Children." The voices of children provide the vehicle for several poems, from "A Story," which appeared in "The Rage for the Lost Penny" (1940) and the powerful "The Prince" and "The Truth" from *The Seven-League Crutches*, to the tripartite title poem of *The Lost World*, in which Jarrell, though speaking as from his own youth, provides an insight into the nature of childhood itself. Like Rilke he writes poems in which dead children speak ("The State" and "Protocols"); poems in which dead warriors speak ("New Georgia" and "Death of the Ball Turret Gunner"); and poems like "Hohensalzburg: Fantastic Variations on a Theme of Romantic Character," in which the dead tell of a transcendence of death in a union with the word, "pure, yearning, unappeasable," that is the principle of the universe.

A wide variety of men speak in Jarrell's poetry, from a sophisticated Robinson Crusoe in "The Island" to the capitalist in "Money," who has learned that his wealth can be an instrument of power whether he spends it or simply gives it away. There is also the affluent apartment dweller in "Hope," restive under protracted oppression by females—mother, wife, cook, maid—and fearful that his son may be doomed to the same fate. By contrast we hear in "A Well-to-Do Invalid" the complaint of a man who enjoys his indignation at what he mistakenly takes to be "the impersonal self-interest" of the wife of an invalid friend and recognizes the real oppressor in that pair only after the wife is dead. These monologues are dramatic in the conventional sense. Two monologues among Jarrell's later poems might be more properly called panegyrics. These are "Woman" in *The Lost World* and the posthumously published "A Man Meets a Woman in the Street." Each is delivered by a speaker who unapologetically adores the woman in his life, and the tone in both has caused commentators to see them as expressions of a deep personal joy—but nonetheless effective as poetry.

UNDERSTANDING RANDALL JARRELL

Actually, in one important respect much of Jarrell's poetry, certainly the best of it, is deeply personal; for whether he was employing the device of monologue or that of the you-address favored by his friend and early mentor Robert Penn Warren or some other strategy, he repeatedly used poetry as an agent of the active sympathy that had created his private universe and that by virtue of its unselfish nature almost always prevented his vision from being egocentric in any pejorative sense. That is, Jarrell habitually moved out to meet the world on its own terms in full empathy. The result was such poems as the much-quoted "A Girl in a Library"; "The Rising Sun," in which he wrote about a Japanese child; "The End of the Rainbow," with its living portrait of a New England spinster in Southern California; and "Lady Bates," a moving address to a little black girl who had died with dignity before she was required to suffer the indignities that life would have imposed upon her.

Jarrell's sympathies went even further, however, to include the animal world that as a child he had identified with in his pet rabbit, Reddy, in the Metro-Goldwyn-Mayer lion that he knew in California, and in the chickens in his grandmother's back yard. At first the animals are incidental, or at best ancillary, to the main scene: the bird in "A Country Life," the imaginary eland in "Seele im Raum," the pet squirrel in "The Night Before the Night Before Christmas," Robinson Crusoe's parrot and goats, the "half-human loves" that comforted him in his isolation, the puppy in "Eighth Air Force," and the magnificent snow leopard that gives distinction to *Little Friend, Little Friend.* In "The Lonely Man," included in *The Woman at the Washington Zoo,* the cats, the collie, and the fat spaniel finally replace human beings in the speaker's interest; and thereafter animals go on to play major roles in *The Lost World.* In the four children's books, published in 1964 and after, animals come fully into their own—rabbits, bats, mockingbird, owl, chipmunk, bear, and lynx. One almost has the feeling that Jarrell resorted to this form not so much because he wanted to write for children as because he saw no other way to provide room for these nonhuman creatures commensurate with his love for them, in his world of stories and poems.

That world, even at the beginning, was one of many territories. In addition to Jarrell's imaginary reconstruction of the South Pacific in the war poems it consists largely of details from his various residences: Southern California, Texas and the Southwest, Nashville, Salzburg, New York, Washington, and Greensboro. It also contains territories provided by his absorption of all of Freud and much of Jung; by his vast reading in poetry and fiction in English; by his lifelong love affair with German literature, and with things German generally; by his almost reverential study of such figures as Proust, Chekhov, Rilke, and Goethe; and by his admiration for Renaissance art and nineteenth-century romantic music (mostly German) with a partiality for Mahler and Richard Strauss. In addition there is the realm provided by Jarrell's dreams, in which he saw himself walking or flying or climbing over vast snowfields (note the snowy landscapes of "90 North," "The Skaters," the last part of "The Night Before the Night Before Christmas," and "Windows"), or spinning among the stars, or wandering in a trackless wood.

The wood seems to have been especially meaningful to him, representing as it does in his finished poems both the unconscious of the individual psyche and the vast realm of being that most people know at best dimly with their senses and rational faculties. Jarrell's wood also coalesces in his mind and in his poems with the dark wood of German märchen, or fairy tale, and thus it brings into his poetry the world of fairy tale, preeminently the story of Hansel and Gretel but other stories as well—Sleeping Beauty, Snow White, Andersen's little mermaid, and Cinderella.[5] Being addicted to things German, Jarrell liked especially the stories of the brothers Grimm, but he was also wary of what such stories could do. This becomes clear in the poem entitled "The Märchen," in which the dark forest is the constant in mankind's long history of awareness, and the fairy stories and folk tales are merely fossils of mankind's early attempts to make sense of it. The story of Hansel was one myth of mankind's savage beginning, his poem tells us; and in time it gave way to others, notably those Asiatic myths of the Scapegoat, "gay with His blood's watered beads," that shaped western Christianity, whetted man's thirst for power, and propelled him into even more savagery. The solution comes suddenly, near the end of the poem, with the assertion that man has never learned what to wish for, leading one to suspect that Jarrell may have been thinking of Rilke's abrupt injunction to the reader midway in the last line of his "Archaic Torso of Apollo": "You must change your life!" Cannot we of the human race, Jarrell's poem asks, put aside the aspirations embodied in our myths and listen to the one valid imperative that comes from our hearts: to submit to the change that is our nature? It is perhaps worth noting here that in Jarrell's treatments the German fairy stories—and all others as well, including Cinderella and the little mermaid—undergo a radical metamorphosis and emerge as new stories, new myths, newly meaningful, The marvelous fairy tales that most people have loved in the hallowed versions in which time has preserved them were, in his view, at best childish delights. Much as he loved them, he valued truth to reality more; and reality in all its sensible manifestations was for him dynamic. This is at least part of the burden of "The House in the Wood," to which he gave a prominent position in his last volume, *The Lost World.*

UNDERSTANDING RANDALL JARRELL

If there is a single theme—assumption would be a better word—that unites Jarrell's achievement, it is his recognition that change, continuous change, is the fundamental characteristic of the universe. Had he been so inclined, he could have found ample support for such a view in the physical sciences or in the works of such process philosophers as Henri Bergson and Alfred North Whitehead, but characteristically he preferred to rely on the authority of the "heart." The world that came daily to his senses was the world that he believed in and gulped with relish, as he said in "Well Water," not expecting or caring to find anything better. Neither the psychiatrist nor the saint in his "Jerome" was able to penetrate much beyond such palatable dailiness, which was something these two could share even with the animals that had become their friends. In one of his most amusing, and most serious, poems Jarrell draws a vivid portrait of his Greensboro paper carrier, who daily "delivers dawn"; and then, speculating playfully on Christian (specifically Moravian) expectations, suggests that on Judgment Day, as he lies cold in his grave and hears the angel approaching, he may well be moved to say, "It is Nestus Gurley." There is, in short, no predictable end to the "dailiness of life."

And yet it is precisely that delicious dailiness that takes away childhood, youth, and eventually physical well-being. In "The Night Before the Night Before Christmas," Jarrell gives a moving account of a young girl who is compelled by circumstances to begin learning the harder aspects of change before she is fully able to deal with them; but he moves the reader almost as much with his portraits of the aging Marschallin in "The Face" and the middle-aged housewife in "Next Day." In two early poems about children in a library he observes that human society through the centuries has filled its books with knowledge about life but has said almost nothing about the change persons must undergo as they live that life; and, as has been noted, in "The Märchen" he earnestly beseeches the reader to put aside false hopes of permanence at the level where flux prevails and listen to the truth that one's heart tells. The penalty for not accepting—or not being *allowed* to accept—the change that life requires is the threat of a death-in-life, a protracted stultification, that causes the woman at the Washington Zoo to cry out in desperation, "Change me, change me!"

Death proper, the physical death that is the natural consequence of life's changes, becomes, in Jarrell's later poems at least, a transition rather than a termination. The dead speak in several of the earlier poems, but there Jarrell is using a palpable device, much like the one used by Edgar Lee Masters in his *Spoon River Anthology.* Precisely what death is a transition to is, understandably, not clear. Jarrell's Prince joins Sleeping Beauty in her eternal slumber, and together they outwit the hunter Death. The vampire lover in "Hohensalzburg: Variations on a Theme of Romantic

Character" assures her captive that in the end "one wakes from everything," and the captive himself looks forward to being forever a "dweller of the Earth, invisible." Goliath in "The Bronze David of Donatello" is dismissed to "blessed death," and the voice in "The House in the Wood" speaks of being held to the breasts of "what was before the world, / And will be after." The intimations of transcendence are too numerous to be dismissed, but they are clearly no more than intimations, and Jarrell does not invite the reader to pursue them. What is certain is that after physical death an image remains with the living. In that way Jarrell's beloved Mama, Pop, and Dandeen, the tall brown aunt, the dog, the rabbit, and the lion of *The Lost World* have all transcended their physical existence and, like the figures in "The Elementary Scene," an early poem, have been blessed by "the future that mends everything." Since the poet Randall Jarrell was their future, the reader of his poem possesses them too.

Yet for Jarrell poetry was never an objective in itself. His purposes were, first, to know the world and, second, to make it known. As he himself put it in answer to a direct question, "It seems to me that the poet's responsibility is to his subject matter, but that one of the determining conditions of the poem is the hypothetical normal audience for which he writes it."[6] Both these factors contributed to that "constant experimentalism" which in 1942 he had declared a primary characteristic of romanticism but which from the beginning had characterized his practice in the craft of poetry. Students of modern poetry have noted evidence of a variety of influences in Jarrell's early work: Auden, whom he admired, deliberately imitated, and planned to write an M.A. thesis about; Tate, an early mentor, and Ransom; Housman, on whose poetry he actually wrote his thesis; and, during the war years, Thomas Hardy. Up through *Blood for a Stranger* Jarrell's work, with regard to both substance and form, was largely exploratory. With the war poetry that made up the two volumes *Little Friend, Little Friend* and *Losses*, the significance of the subject matter, as far as he was concerned, was never in question. There Jarrell simply concentrated on making the form appropriate. By the time he came to do the poems for *Seven-League Crutches*, he had settled upon his proper subjects and learned to control his form.

More important, he had found a mode that was distinctively his: part dramatic monologue, part dialogue, part direct address to the subject at hand; all delivered in a form that was flexible without being entirely free. The most common line was a loose iambic with five beats; but the length could vary as necessary, and occasional rhymes and repetitions gave coherence and emphasized the emergent meanings. Toward the end he began to make use of terza rima to strengthen the coherence of longer poems—for example, in the three parts of "The Lost World" and in "The Owl's Bedtime Story," which was published as a part of the children's story *Fly by Night*. One of his last poems, "The Player Piano," is written in five-line un-rhymed stanzas, a strategy that he had employed as early as 1940 ("Eine kleine Nachtmusik") and used occasionally thereafter throughout his career—for example, in "The Lonely Man" (five-line stanzas), "Next Day" (six-line stanzas), and "The House in the Wood" (two-line stanzas).

During the early and middle years of his career Jarrell's syntax sometimes tended to be tortuous, particularly in poems like "The Märchen," in which the progression of the thought was intended to be associative rather than logical. Frequently, however, the difficulties are only apparent, as in dramatic poems like "A Quilt-Pattern" and "The End of the Rainbow," both of which tend to come clear when read aloud, as they were intended to be. In fact, in all of Jarrell's work the language is colloquial, that of the spoken word; and toward the end of his life the sound of the language, always in his mind's ear, more often than not determined the disposition of terms and the shape of the units. From beginning to end, however, Jarrell had two authorities and only two: the subject before him in all its sensible immediacy and the "hypothetical" auditor. Critics are only now beginning to recognize how successful he was in bringing these two together.

UNDERSTANDING RANDALL JARRELL

Notes

1. Reprinted in *Kipling, Auden & Co.* (New York: Farrar, Straus, 1980) 76–83.

2. For a good discussion of Jarrell's modernism, or postmodernism, see Jerome Mazzaro, *Postmodern American Poetry* (Champaign: University of Illinois Press, 1980) 32–58. An excellent general account of Jarrell's work is William H. Pritchard's essay "Randall Jarrell: Poet-Critic," *The American Scholar* 52 (1982–83): 67–77; reprinted in *Critical Essays on Randall Jarrell*, ed. Suzanne Ferguson (Boston: G. K. Hall, 1983) 120–39.

3. For an account of Jarrell's debt to Rilke—one that he never tired of repaying—see Charlotte Beck, "Unicorn to Eland: The Rilkean Spirit in the Poetry of Randall Jarrell," *Critical Essays on Jarrell* 191–202. Beck deals at length with the dramatic monologues in her book *World and Lives: The Poetry of Randall Jarrell* (Port Washington, N.Y.: Associated Faculty Press, 1983) 25–68.

4. John Crowe Ransom, "The Rugged Way of Genius," *Randall Jarrell 1914–1965*, ed. Robert Lowell, Peter Taylor, and Robert Penn Warren (New York: Farrar, Straus, 1967) 173.

5. Stanley Kunitz quotes approvingly Karl Shapiro's observation that the subtitle of Jarrell's work might well be "Hansel and Gretel in America," *Randall Jarrell 1914–1965* 100. See also Helen Hagenbüchle's essay "Blood for the Muse: A Study of the Poetic Process in Randall Jarrell's Poetry," *Critical Essays on Jarrell* 101–19.

6. "Answers to Questions," *Kipling, Auden & Co.* 170.

CHAPTER TWO

The Earlier Poems

I n 1969, four years after Jarrell's death, the publishing house of Farrar, Straus & Giroux brought out *Randall Jarrell: The Complete Poems*.[1] This version of the poetry is probably close to Jarrell's final intention, and it is the version that most people read. Thus except as otherwise noted, *The Complete Poems* will be the edition referred to in this chapter and in chapter 5.

Jarrell's first four volumes of poetry were *Blood for a Stranger* (1942), *Little Friend, Little Friend* (1945), *Losses* (1948), and *The Seven-League Crutches* (1951). His *Selected Poems*, published in 1955 and reprinted without change in *Complete Poems*, includes ten from the first of these, twenty-four from *Little Friend, Little Friend*, all but two from *Losses*, all but one from *Seven-League Crutches*, and two unpublished poems, making a total of ninety-four. These are arranged in two large groups. The first is devoted to topics and themes that had dominated *Blood for a*

Stranger—the perceptions of childhood, the precarious state of western civilization, human loneliness, and the significance of dreams; these later reemerged in *Seven-League Crutches*, supported and augmented there by a new preoccupation with woman and the feminine sensibility and by a vigorous interest in the graphic and plastic arts, in fairy tales, and in the culture of Central Europe. The second group consists of those poems that reflect Jarrell's experiences, real and imaginary, during World War II. Only four poems from *Seven-League Crutches* appear in this second group and none at all from *Blood for a Stranger*. In addition, in an introduction Jarrell gives commentary for some of the poems—a practice he had initiated at the conclusion of *Losses* but abandoned for *The Woman at the Washington Zoo* and *The Lost World*. Even so, he continued to provide "prose to go along with the poems" in the succession of readings that he gave during the last years of his life.

Jarrell was an astute critic of his own work, and a reading of *Selected Poems* provides an impression of professional maturity that is at variance with the impression one gets from reading the first four volumes in their entirety and in the order of their publication. In the 1955 volume Jarrell presented most of the poems he definitely wished to preserve, some of these in revised form, and arranged them so that the poems could reinforce and illuminate one another. The result

THE EARLIER POEMS

is a body of poetry that is a tribute to the genius of both the early and the mature Randall Jarrell and one that stands in *The Complete Poems* as a worthy companion to *The Woman at the Washington Zoo* and *The Lost World*.[2]

Jarrell subdivided each of the two divisions of *Selected Poems* into groups of from four to ten poems each, and to each group he gave a descriptive title. The first group, called "Lives," contains ten poems, all taken from *Losses* and *The Seven-League Crutches*, that are easily among his best. All but one are monologues, a device that Jarrell favored throughout his career and the one that dominated *The Lost World*. The speaker in two of the monologues is a woman, and the focus of attention in four others is on a female. This strategy, too, is an anticipation of later work. Jarrell was always, like Eliot's Tiresias, "throbbing between two lives," one male and one female; but here in the earlier pieces the ambivalence passes as little more than a writer's alternation of voices, and the sex of the speaker in most of these poems is scarcely relevant. The dominant subject in them, regardless of persona, is the mystery of human existence—life and death, and the poet's acceptance of both. It would be difficult to choose a group of poems better suited to serve as an introduction to Jarrell's work.

A good poem to begin with comes from *Seven-League Crutches*, "A Conversation with the Devil," in which Jarrell deals with his chosen role as poet for the intellectually elite.[3] The poet, like Faust, has made a pact with the Devil, here identified as "some poor empty part" of the poet's own psyche, whereby he will agree "Neither to live/Nor ask for life" in return for a creative man's privilege of seeing things not only as they are but as they might be. The Devil tempts him to regret his rejection of the common man's world, concluding feebly with Ludwig Wittgenstein's "The world divides into facts." But the poet stands fast, and the Devil retires sadly to the annihilation disguised as reality that he has successfully sold to countless others. The poet stands free, liberated by the choice that he exercised in his initial sacrifice.

An even more impressive poem on the same theme is "The Knight, Death, and the Devil," a meditation on the engraver, Albrecht Dürer's masterpiece, in which a Christian knight moves steadily toward his goal in defiance of a Devil, half goat and half swine, lurking behind him and the threats of a Death menacing with an hourglass at his side. Jarrell's knight looks steadily past both specters, not at some vision of Christian fulfillment such as one imagines Dürer must have had in mind, but at a vision which the man's own look creates ("completes itself"); and the body of the knight, realistically portrayed by the engraver in contrast to the allegorical figures of Death and the Devil, affirms its being by simple existence.

THE EARLIER POEMS

Another poem in this first group, "Lady Bates," deals more forthrightly with the fact of death. During the composition of this one Jarrell may have remembered Ransom's "Bells for John Whiteside's Daughter," in which the death of an innocent child profoundly "vexes" the adults who have come dutifully to pay their respects.[4] Here the dead innocent is Lady Bates, a little black girl, who sleeps in a "clay cave" near the spot where she used to eat blackberries. The speaker does not sentimentalize. She is, after all, only "poor black trash" whom the wind blew away by mistake. But he dignifies her by imagining in the child's terms the cosmic significance of her brief life and the circumstances of her passing: how the Trinity sang "like a quartet" about the suddenness of her death, about the pair of angels ("one coal-black, one high-yellow") they sent to fetch her soul, and about how Death hypnotically immobilized her in a sleep that is more like liberation than annihilation.

The same speaker contemplates a dozing girl in "A Girl in a Library," the poem that Jarrell chose to stand first in his collection; but this time his compassionate voice is contrasted with that of Alexander Pushkin's Tatyana from *Eugene Onegin*, who sees the girl as a fat little peasant dreaming impossible dreams. The speaker knows better. The girl is not dreaming: her life itself is a sleeping, to be interrupted only fitfully in moments of little more than half-awareness of the full life that could be hers if only her very human flesh were not congenitally reluctant to put on spirit. And yet Jarrell does not reject this child of common humanity as Tatyana is inclined to do; he loves her for her female humanness, for the woman's life she inevitably must live through whether or not she ever stops to reflect about it, and for the sacrifice she as someone's "Spring Queen" is destined to become in the natural course of things. The most moving thing about both poems, however, is the speaker's compassionate perception of the humanity that involves everybody, the alert as well as the dull, and the finality of the common sleep that concludes the dreaming for all alike.

Two of the poems in this group, both from *Seven-League Crutches*, are monologues spoken by women. "Face" begins with a quotation from Hugo von Hofmannsthal's libretto for Richard Strauss's *Der Rosenkavalier: "Die alte Frau, die alte Marschallin,"* words that the Marschallin in her wistful meditation on her youth that is slipping away feels will be said of her before long. Jarrell's aging woman, however, has no musical accompaniment to soften the harshness of her perceptions or the painful directness of the language he gives her to express them. She has changed, inwardly as well as outwardly; and the fact of loss, which she has done nothing to deserve except to live through her days, outrages her. "It's not *right*," she says, perceiving at last that merely being alive has its

THE EARLIER POEMS

terror. The speaker in "Seele im Raum" ("Soul in Space") has undergone a period of mental illness; imagined that she owned an eland, an African antelope that one seldom sees except in zoos; and then, aided by the patience and love of her family, come back to normal perception again. The title of the poem has been borrowed from one of Rilke's; the substance is analogous to that of another Rilke poem, in which perfectly sane people have lovingly created the imaginary unicorn, an idealized creature, quite unlike the ungainly but gentle eland. Both Rilke's and Jarrell's poems deal with the reality and dignity of the products of human creativity. The eland, like the unicorn, is at once a product and a generator of love. The woman begins to understand that when, browsing through a German dictionary, she discovers that *elend* in German means "wretched" and sees that although the imaginary animal grew out of her great pain, it prompted husband and children to countless acts of tenderness and nourished in her a capacity for affection. Thus a measure of the fulfillment in her life will consist in being able in old age to look back with satisfaction at having owned the eland, who gave back to her the being she had given it and allowed her figuratively to pat the live hard side of its neck.

Jarrell's optimism here does not extend beyond the grave. The section concludes with still another poem from *Seven-League Crutches*, "The Night Before the Night Before Christmas," at 375 lines the longest of Jarrell's poems, in which he deals with a young person's encounter with the fact that death is omnipresent in human life. A parenthetical subtitle gives the date 1934, and the central figure in the poem is a girl, about fourteen, who is interested in Marxism (as Jarrell himself was at that time), and is reading widely and voraciously and firing questions at the universe. She has felt deeply the death two years earlier of her youthful mother, whom she has come to resemble; and she now lives in an apartment with her father, her aunt, and a brother, who also seems to be dying. Like any adolescent she has a faltering sense of her own identity; but she aspires to be a Mary in the world rather than a Martha, and she has tried to assert her budding individuality in the modest presents she has been able to buy for her brother ("improving and delightful things"), aunt, and father. Her father, she recognizes, were he female, would be one of the Marthas; but then he was sympathetic when a squirrel she befriended disappeared from the park and did not return. Thoughts of the squirrel bring into focus questions she has been asking about the certitudes her Christian world has proffered her. Squirrels have nothing to lose but their lives, she thinks, as she drifts off to sleep and, troubled with doubts, dreams of flying out over the snow-covered world: above her a universe of galaxies, backed with a mysterious blackness that shows only

THE EARLIER POEMS

her own face, reflected as in a mirror; below, snowy fields, lovely but with no angels in them, nothing indeed that knows it is Christmas. Recalling the story of Hansel and Gretel, she imagines that her dying brother is with her as they attempt to retrace their steps homeward by the crumbs of tears they have dropped. The frame-story shifts to that of the babes in the wood, dead and buried here under snow rather than leaves; then they are both flying, upward and homeward, recalling their lives. The girl remembers the hopeful assurance in Sidney Carton's dying words, clasps her brother's hand, and begins to cry. One suspects that her worst human fears are being realized: in this dream of death family and friends, except for the tenuous hold she maintains on her brother, are all gone; her hopes of salvation by learning and sophistication no longer have any relevance, even if they ever had any validity; and all she has been told about religion is, as she suspected, illusory. Among Jarrell's earlier poems this is by far the most ambitious. It does not entirely succeed; but what it achieves is far too valuable to be discarded, and one suspects Jarrell would have revised it in later years, had he not chosen, in effect, to write the poem again in the "Hope" that appears in *The Woman at the Washington Zoo*.

The next section of *Selected Poems*, appropriately entitled "Dream-Work," presents poems that involve the exploration and exploitation of dreams. Jarrell's lifelong preoccupation with Freud ensured that such subjects would recur frequently throughout the entire canon, but at least two of the examples in this group are among his best. One of these, a relatively simple example, is "The Black Swan," a poem reminiscent of the early Yeats in subject and imagery, though not in control. Here in five five-line unrhymed stanzas a girl expresses her longing to join her dead sister, whom she thinks of as having been transformed into a swan. The line between dream and actuality disappears in this poem, as the girl hears the night cries of the other swans and finally, feeling the caress of her sister's black wing, joins her in death.[5]

A more typical poem is "A Quilt-Pattern," in which a young boy, sick in bed, falls asleep and dreams a version of the Hansel and Gretel story. The quilt on his bed has a tree of life pattern on it, which may have something to do with the boy's interpretation of the story as a reenactment of Adam's expulsion from the Garden. Falling through "leagues of space/ Into the oldest tale of all," he sees himself at first in a steamy place where he is surrounded by hutches filled with rabbits, all destined to be killed for their fur. The boy, who has in him Adam's proclivities for both good and evil ("Good me, bad me"), knows that he in his fur jacket has been benefiting thoughtlessly from the death of these creatures but nevertheless identifies with them and shares the blackberries that they nibble

THE EARLIER POEMS

through the wire mesh of their cages. The nearby house seems to coalesce with the oppressive aspect of his mother ("the dead mother"); at any rate, that is where she bathes (bastes) Bad me, sticks a washcloth in his mouth, and seems intent on devouring him altogether. In the next section, however, the situation reverses itself in conformity with the tale, which has the children (combined here as one child with two aspects) nibble at the house, this time identifiable both as the mother, the source of life, and as the forbidden tree in Adam's garden. Suddenly the meaning of the steam that surrounded the rabbit hutches becomes clear: it is the steam of the oven, now hot and ready to receive the "bread," and the house urges her nibbling "mouse" to slip it in. There follows the stratagem of the children whereby the house or mother, now identified also as the "Other" (a meaningful rhyme), is forced screaming to take the place in the oven intended for "Bad me, good me." These two smile at each other timidly as the dreaming child, reintegrated and wiser, wakes to hear his mother calling, "How is my little mouse? Awake?" feigns sleep, and resolves to preserve his independence of that nightmare forever.[6]

"The Island" differs from the other dream poems in the group. For one thing, it is more formally organized. Like "The Black Swan" it consists of five-line stanzas; but the lines in "The Island" are varied against an implied norm of iambic pentameter, and the second and fifth lines of the first three stanzas rhyme. Thereafter the rhyming, like the meter, becomes irregular and unpredictable; but the careful ear can still hear the echoing in *stars*, *Mars*, and *scars* and recognize the repetitions of the word *sea*. These effects, subtly suggesting a relaxation of formal restraints, reinforce another distinctive aspect of the poem: its affirmation that the nighttime dream—here Crusoe's dream of European civilization—is little more than a discredited memory, a collection of fairy tales that dissolves with the dawn. Life too diminishes: man, parrot, and goat grow old and "wait in their grove for death." The "unguessed abyss," however, the salt sea, "summer's witless stare"—these things endure and ultimately prevail.

The section "The Wide Prospect" liberates the reader from the solipsistic cell in which "Dream-Work" has temporarily kept him and directs his gaze to a world outside the psyche. For Jarrell the reality of that external world, whether seen or unseen, was an article of faith. Most of the poems in this group are from a section in *The Seven-League Crutches* called "Europe," which Jarrell had seen for the first time in 1948 when he taught at the Salzburg Summer Seminar in American Civilization. These he combined with other "European" poems from *Blood for a Stranger* and *Losses* to give an unusual set of perspectives on the relation of the individual to externality. The first poem, "The Orient Express," takes views from a train as a metaphor for the human tendency to accept surfaces as total reality. The reader is invited to look at the little villages as they slide past, the fields of grain, the men and the women, "a path through a wood full of lives," and in the glare of daylight to feel safe from the troubling complexity, the "unwanted life," that lies behind and beyond appearances. In the second poem, "A Game at Salzburg," Jarrell demands almost explicitly a recognition of the dignity of the world in its totality. The metaphor here is that of a game German adults sometimes play with small children. "Here am I," the child says timidly, and the adult responds, modulating his voice as he does so with a positive cadence, "There are *you*." The world, the poem says, is a child who plays that game with all human creatures, demanding attention and love, and all the while, like the child, more than a little fearful that those creatures will not or cannot respond.

The world in its totality, in Jarrell's view, includes all places and all times—past, present, and future—flowing together in essential unity. The extensiveness of it becomes clear in the poem "An English Garden in Austria," in which a speaker, still under the spell of a performance of *Der Rosenkavalier*, uses the framework of von Hofmannsthal's bittersweet vision of life's continual change to unify his perception of the dissolving and reshaping of European culture. The gothic

English garden in neoclassical Vienna is a romantic intrusion that once foreshadowed and now calls to mind the passage from Rousseau to the French Revolution to *Werther* to Napoleon and thence to Hitler and Stalin. Jarrell has given this poem the longest prefatory note in his introduction, and the reader needs little more than that and a rough knowledge of the opera to see him through. It helps to know that both the discredited boor Baron Ochs von Lerchenau and the aging Marschallin accept the inevitable fact of change regretfully but with good grace.

The prospect widens in yet another direction in "A Soul," a poem that reinterprets Andersen's "The Little Sea Maid." Interpretations of Jarrell's version have differed considerably. In Andersen's tale the mermaid belongs to the order of nature and can achieve transcendence of that order only if she can win the love of a human being with his immortal soul. Quinn sees the poem as a happy celebration of the reunion of mortal and immortal, something that did not take place in Andersen's version; but Ferguson, sensing a lack of joyousness in the man, sees in their meeting the man's sober quest for individuation in the Jungian *anima* and suggests that the mermaid may also symbolize the Freudian id, a likely possibility in view of Jarrell's marked preference for Freud.[7] In any case, the meeting, briefly but movingly presented in an exchange between the two, seems to be joyous only for the maid.

THE EARLIER POEMS

Clearly this meeting is only the latest of a number of inconclusive ones, and it does not promise to be any more conclusive than the others. "Many times I had thought thee lost, / My poor soul, forever," she says in the last lines; but the irony in her words is patent. The man will return to the castle, where "someone is singing," and his estrangement from the fulfillment of his being will continue. His emptiness is another example of the "unwilling sadness" that the viewer sensed behind almost everything as he watched from the window of the Orient Express.

"A Rhapsody on Irish Themes" is among the poems that John Crowe Ransom singled out for praise, and as an example of craftsmanship it is surely one of the most arresting pieces in *The Seven-League Crutches*.[8] It is also unusual as being one of the few poems in which Jarrell suppressed his sympathetic impulses and wrote sarcastically of a subject he had decided to dislike. The speaker has returned to his geographic roots and found mainly decadence and ignorance. He tells the old woman who tries to sell him a cheap embroidered handkerchief made "by the Little People," "I hold nothing/ Against you but what you are." She is the Circe who can only corrupt, and Ulysseslike he makes haste to sail away from an island that by rights should have been his Ithaca.

"The Memoirs of Glückel of Hameln," an earlier poem, puts him on more congenial ground. Jarrell had a fondness for writing poems about and sometimes, as here, *to* authors whose books he had read with interest; Glückel, an eighteenth-century German Jew who wrote his memoirs in Yiddish, was one of these. The details of Glückel's book had nothing to do with Jarrell's own forebears, of course, and for the most part the events described in it bored him: business transactions, marriages, deaths, trivia of various kinds, with money and God being "The necessities that governed every act." Moreover, there was nothing whatever in the book about such intellectual giants of the time as Newton, Leibnitz, Mandeville, and Pope, figures whom Jarrell would normally have been willing to pay attention to. Glückel, however, for all his tediousness, reminds the reader that the main body of any period in history is composed principally of the kind of perceptions he records in his memoirs. Thus for practical purposes, the data of Glückel's past are the data of everybody's past, the continuing substance of which all people are a part and which will be shared by all those who come after.

"The Märchen," another early piece (this time from *Losses*), also deals with the life human beings share with their forebears. This poem, with its remarkable concatenation of allusions and its apparently deliberate avoidance of clear connections and transitions is easily one of the most inaccessible that Jarrell ever wrote. Consequently the impact of it, even on the

THE EARLIER POEMS

most informed readers, has probably fallen considerably short of what Jarrell must have hoped for.[9] The
subject of the poem seems to be the attempt by North
European man, presented by Jarrell as a series of rein-
carnations of the Hansel figure, to know himself in a
world which from time immemorial he has thought of
as alien territory, the domain of hostile forces, mali-
cious gods, devils, tyrants. The means to mankind's
knowledge has always been the succession of myths or
fictions in which through century after century his
seers, poets, and tale-tellers have attempted to imagine, embody, and make visible the powers he would
either defeat or learn to manipulate. Thus he has
known, or thought he has known, the ancient Nordic
pantheon, the devil in various guises, the scapegoat
Christ imported from warmer climates, and a succession of giants, warlocks, and unburied dead. European man's addresses to these powers have been
usually the articulation of wishes, which in his view
were sometimes granted and sometimes not. In the
speaker's view, however, events have followed their
own course quite without reference to supplications.
Have we not learned, he cries out at the end, to put
aside the tales that have shaped our lives and listen to
our own hearts, which entertain death as a normal in-
habitant rather than the perennial enemy, and which
tell us man's natural mode of life is not to dominate
but like that of all the humbler creatures to change,

UNDERSTANDING RANDALL JARRELL

metamorphose, and accommodate to a world of eternal process, unobscured by human illusions and nightmares?

The last selection in "The Wide Prospect" addresses itself to the final stage in the human accommodation to process. This is "Hohensalzburg: Fantastic Variations on a Theme of Romantic Character," another poem from *The Seven-League Crutches* and one of the most memorable of Jarrell's poems from any period. The castle referred to in the title is the one that broods over the Austrian city of Salzburg, where Jarrell spent a summer in 1948, and the fictional plot of the poem is the seduction of a male visitor to the castle environs by the spirit of a vampire maiden who haunts it. As Beck notes in her discussion of the poem, the dialogue that one hears between the male narrator and the maiden is actually subsumed into a monologue by the male visitor, and with good reason; for the underlying action of the poem is, in Jungian terms, the integration of the male consciousness with its complementary anima, or female component, and the merging of both with the primal unity that transcends time and place.[10] Thus the male narrator can speak for the maid because at the time of the poem he has already united himself with her—in the fiction of the poem, joined his blood with hers—and so is both man and maid. Behind this fantastic but credible narration, and made manifest by it, is the human yearning for

THE EARLIER POEMS

immortality. The narrator recalls for the girl how she and her godmother discussed her youthful wishes over evening tea and discovered that no wish she might make could be forever save one: the wish for invisibility, as the girl puts it. The meaning of that wish becomes clear as the reader learns that behind all the visibilia, behind all the things people might wish for, is the "word we have never understood," that "steady sound" in which life, death, past, and future are lost. In the end, the spirit maiden promises, one wakes, or escapes, from particulars and becomes a part of the earthly permanence—"a dweller of the Earth, invisible." Thus, one might say, this poem ends in death redeemed, and "The Wide Prospect" as a whole, with an affirmation of the infinity of this world.

For the next section Jarrell begins to dip again into his earlier collections—*Blood for a Stranger, Little Friend, Little Friend,* and *Losses.* The title, "Once Upon a Time," may be thought to refer to Jarrell's use of märchen in two of the poems or to his depiction of children in the library in two others; but more likely he is again referring to the human disposition that he saw as both revealed and confirmed by many of the fictions human beings inherit—that is, a disposition to resist the notion that change is the essential mode of their being. In the poem entitled "The Märchen," as has been noted, Jarrell implicitly deplored the constrictive authority that recurring myth ("once upon a time") has imposed on the race; here in the earlier of his two poems about the library he deplores it specifically. The lives of the young people in "Children Selecting Books in a Library" are as full of "sorcerers and ogres" as the lives of adults are, and they are just as helpless in the face of "the capricious infinite." Hence they read, forever hopeful of answers or cures or means of escape, grasping at opportunities to change momentarily their own sorrows for those of another, all the while fretting with their own concerns and resisting adamantly the imperative to change, a word Jarrell uncharacteristically presents in capitals: CHANGE. "The Carnegie Library, Juvenile Division" carries substantially the same burden. The collection there is characterized as a "fire-sale of the centuries," documents which have made civilized humanity what it is but which are of themselves powerless to reveal to humanity its nature. These can provide knowledge of many things but not the crucial knowledge of how to change and achieve natural fulfillment.

The folly of settling for the patterns of fulfillment that the world provides, all of which are predicated on the desirability of preserving the integrity of self, is nowhere more cruelly revealed than in the presence of death, which renders all such projects, goals, and achievements meaningless. Jarrell deals with this matter on two poems, one from *The Seven-League Crutches* and the other from *Losses*. In the first, "The Sleeping

Beauty: Variation of the Prince," he presents an ingenious variation on the Grimms' tale of the prince's triumph over the apparent death of the sleeping girl. As in the original, the young man makes his way through the thicket of thorns to find a community of sleepers frozen in the moment of their enchantment; but instead of waking the princess to make her his bride and live happily ever after in an impossible dream of an unchanging future, he gently touches his lips to hers and then lies down by her side, placing the sword of Death between them. In the millennia to come, he says, they will sleep undisturbed, waking for no one except the hunter, Death himself, whom they will also persuade to join them in their transcendence of mortality in a "last long world." The patent absurdity of this new resolution to the tale only underscores and makes visible the normally undetected absurdity of the resolution in the original version.

The second poem, however, originally "The Child of Courts" but now simply called "The Prince," presents what might be considered a step toward the acceptance of a universe involved in perpetual change. It is nonetheless disquieting. A young child, put to bed by his mother, begins to imagine a presence nearby in the darkness of something or someone unknown and fancies that it may be the friend or relative whose death recently so distressed him that his parents gave him a pet rabbit by way of consolation.

UNDERSTANDING RANDALL JARRELL

When the boy puts out his hand and finds nothing there, he is even more disturbed and begins to weep at the thought of the annihilation that he suddenly realizes death must be ("there are no ghosts"). Then he asks, in terms that are no less dignified for being childish, whether his death, too, will mean no more than the death of a rabbit.

Another poem in this section, "The Skaters," taken unchanged from *Blood for a Stranger*, presents in images that are arresting but difficult to interpret the plight of modern man who tries, with his dispositions and predilections intact, to comprehend the process of the cosmic dance. Metrically this poem is characteristic of the experiments that Jarrell engaged in during the early part of his career. Here he presents nine four-line stanzas, with lines for the most part in iambic trimeter but dramatically and appropriately varied with an occasional tetrameter, and with the second and fourth lines of the first eight stanzas linked by either assonance or consonance, leaving the finality of a full rhyme to the ninth stanza alone. In subject matter the poem is faintly reminiscent of the seventeenth-century Henry Vaughan's "The World" ("I saw eternity the other night"); here, however, the ring is not part of the kingdom of God but simply a procession of skaters, disembodied spirits, speeding through the endless passages of a frigid and sterile eternity. The speaker joins them, attempts a liaison with one of the skaters, and then suggests that the two block out in some fashion a "shelter from this endless night." His ignorance and folly become evident as the procession, with himself now inextricably a part of it, continues relentlessly its descent into the abyss.

Several examples of a very different kind of poem that Jarrell was also publishing in the forties are included in the next group, named after the first proposition of Wittgenstein's *Tractatus*, "The World Is Everything That Is the Case." Among these poems is an amusing dramatic monologue by a religious fundamentalist who, having bought Venetian blinds, shoes, and a pronouncing bible from the Sears catalog, expresses a mixture of fascination and fear of judgment by fire at seeing the "wilderness" of women's underwear displayed there. Another monologue, "Money," presents an aesthetically insensitive financier who has run out of things to buy but has come to enjoy the power that money confers, whether one buys things with it or gives it away. "The Empancipators," from *Little Friend, Little Friend*, suggests that the financier is all too representative of a world for which men like Galileo, Newton, and Giordano Bruno, who were geniuses, committed to acquiring knowledge that might make men free, risked their reputations and even their lives. Now, centuries later, the purely intellectual triumphs of these giants "metamorphose into use"; all their successors can understand or wish for apparently is Trade, and the emancipators have emancipated no one. There are those, however, who achieve nothing even by way of Trade, and these have a special kind of vanity all their own. Jarrell has provided a representative of these, the world's "losers," in an Audenlike poem, "Hope," in which the speaker never quite gives up expecting to receive some announcement of material good fortune, and so stops Time twice on five days during the week and once on Saturday, to look hopefully in "Folly's mailbox."[11]

The vanity of a more serious kind of wish is presented in a quite beautiful translation of Tristan Corbière's "Le Poète Contumace," in which the poet, housed in a crumbling tower on the coast of Brittany, with only a hammock to give him ease and a hurdy-gurdy and a spaniel to keep him company, draws upon his talents to re-create in a letter a companion who will live with him again, rejoice in the Breton landscape with him, and bring life and love to his days and nights.[12] At the end, predictably, that hope vanishes, even as the poet's love of life has substantially all but vanished; and he tears the letter into bits and throws it out the window into the fog.

So with all lives, Jarrell seems to say in another poem, "A Utopian Journey," first published in *Blood for a Stranger* as "The Long Vacation." In that piece a physician's patient, seriously ill, goes through the long process of ensuring that he will be able "to go on being"—the initial visit to the office, then the hospital or sanitorium, the tests, the treatments, and finally the convalescence—only to discover in the end that he has learned nothing, not in this experience nor in all his experiences preceding, and that all his life has been simply a matter of staying alive in order to find at last the way to the exit. Another poem from that same early volume, "Variations," is equally somber. The variations referred to here are life stories: first, the perennial story of characters in a Punch and Judy show; next, the life of the son of God on earth; then the life that a child fashions out of the nightmares of his existence and his nursery tales; and finally the routine lives of all men, white, black, and yellow. For all these the world has one sentence, signifying the meaninglessness of their actions: "Child, you will not be missed."

Apparently the trick of living may be in learning what *not* to expect or ask for. That, at least, is a significant implication of the most impressive poem in this group, "The Snow-Leopard." The poem has no plot. It simply presents the animal, beautiful in its perfect adaptation to the environment it has inherited and as heartless and incurious as the crystal clouds that float beneath his gaze, staring at a merchant caravan of yaks far below, "raiders of the unminding element." The caravan moves with painful slowness in that rarefied air, where it does not belong and but for the necessity of trade and its great expectations would never have come. The leopard, "cold, fugitive, secure," looks indifferently ("sleepily") at all the world he knows, purrs, and waves his six-foot tail.

A final poem from *Blood for a Stranger*, "90 North," is one of the most memorable of Jarrell's early poems, and the one that contains what is probably, after his conclusion to "The Death of the Ball Turret Gunner," his most frequently quoted line. The title refers to the North Pole, where the dreaming child arrives after clambering "up the globe's impossible sides." For children of Jarrell's generation reaching the North Pole (or the South Pole for that matter) had meaning as an ultimate adventure of the human spirit; and for a moment the child dreams that the achievement of that adventure is his. He stands at the point where all lines converge and the only direction left is south. His satisfaction quickly vanishes, however, as he perceives that the pole of his own existence is like that. At the pole of his life, too, all the lines and winds converge, but they do so in a meaningless whirlpool. He must live and die by accident, and whatever happens he must remain alone. The knowledge that he gained from his adventure in living, "wrung [in pain] from the darkness," is what the world calls wisdom. He knows better: "It is pain."

This affirmation, "It is pain," one that has found its way into collections of quotations, cannot be used to characterize all the poems in the first half of Jarrell's 1955 collection, but nothing in the collection contradicts it. Human lives are meaningless, he seems to say, if measured by the foolish patterns human beings have created for themselves. But true self-knowledge, presumably the product of such undirected maturation as nonhuman creatures enjoy, which brings the serenity of a snow leopard and the transcendence of the fantastic emancipated ghost of the Hohensalzburg, this is something that human beings achieve only with great suffering. In "The Breath of Night," one of the poems of the final group in part I of *Selected Poems*, the nonhuman world is presented in images of rural life—fox cubs rolling together in the ferns, deer, rabbits, a cock, an owl, a pair of stars. All these, the poem says, are swept by the eternal "Strife" that turns the universe; yet death does not preoccupy their thoughts, and their joy in life for the most part more than compensates for the hostile forces they must somehow come to terms with as long as they expect to go on living. All the other poems in the group present images or anticipations of death, a natural phenomenon but one which sophisticated man anticipates with dread and which he regards as focal point for whatever meaning the course of his life may achieve.

As in previous poems, many of Jarrell's human characters achieve nothing. For example, in "La Belle au Bois Dormant," Sleeping Beauty returns as a woman murdered by her lover, dismembered, and stuffed in a trunk. "What wish, what keen pain has enchanted her/ To this cold period?" the speaker asks; but for this sleeper ("alas! not beautiful") no prince, no hunter will come. Her death has been as meaningless as it was gruesome, and the world is almost ready to say to her, as it said to the "variations" in a preceding poem, "Child, you will not be missed."

In "A Story," a remarkable monologue in sestina form, from *Blood for a Stranger*, a young boy left at a boarding school finds satisfaction neither in recollections of home nor in the prospects of his present situation, to which apparently he will never adjust. Thus having exhausted, he thinks, the possibilities of achieving a meaningful existence, he turns his mind to the one remaining alternative and contemplates suicide. In "Loss" the reader is back in the animal kingdom, as the speaker in the poem contemplates a dead bird and asks, in effect, the question with which Villon tormented posterity, "Where are the snows of yesteryear?" The dead have no answers, of course, to such questions; but Jarrell lets the speaker in his translation of Corbière's *Rondels pour après*, entitled "Afterwards," suggest them as he addresses the dead child, the "little thief of starlight," who bears lightly his "load of everlastings" and mocks the self-assured grownups who "think you're dead." Again, as in the poem "Lady Bates," the death of a child throws into question the validity of our categories, and we are "vexed" beyond endurance at the affront to the order we have so painstakingly constructed for our human world.

A resolution comes in a poem included in *Losses*, "The Place of Death," a poem reminiscent of Tate's "Ode to the Confederate Dead." As in Tate's poem, the setting is a cemetery, here an American public cemetery with its customary furniture: a plaited wicker wreath with the green varnish on it still wet enough to catch and hold gnats, a fruit jar with fading flowers in it, a stone angel staring at a stone Bible, a squirrel to catch the eye and a woodpecker to break the stillness. Into the scene comes a student, reading and meditating, as the youthful Jarrell himself did, on the philosophy of Spinoza, which has taught him that all things are transient modes of the "seeding and inhuman Substance" that constitutes the universe. In Spinoza's view all boundaries are temporary—including those that define the bodies buried beneath the mounds and those defining the souls that presumably inhabited those bodies—are are destined to fade into the eternal continuum of Being. The mourners who thought otherwise of the one recently dead are all gone now, and the only mourners remaining are the squirrel, the woodpecker, and the gnats, who, because of the wet varnish, have dead of their own to consider. The student falls asleep and with him the spirit of Spinoza, the part-time lens grinder; but as he dreams, the angel seems to whisper a paraphrase of another angel's words to the Marys who visited the tomb of their risen Lord, "He is not here—see, see, he is not here." These words point to the human hope of resurrection, of a renewal of life beyond death; but the nonhuman creatures who play out their lives in this place where the human fear of death is signed in grassy mounds, statuary, and flowers know that life, death, and resurrection are all part of one eternal process. Only man, the victim of his myths, is miserable in his ignorant reverence for self and his stubborn resistance to change.

The War Poems

Most of the forty-four war poems in the second part of *Selected Poems* were published originally in *Little Friend, Little Friend* and *Losses*. Four came from *The Seven-League Crutches*: "Transient Barracks," "The Truth," "Good-bye, Wendover; Goody-bye, Mountain Home," and "Terms." Two poems, "The Survivor among Graves" and "A War," were new.

Jarrell never saw combat during World War II and never served overseas. Having failed to qualify for ferry-pilot training, he enlisted in the army air force as a private and served for a time as a link trainer instructor. When the need for that duty diminished, he qualified as a celestial-navigation tower operator. Nevertheless, the poems that Jarrell wrote during this

THE EARLIER POEMS

period in his life have enabled him to stand with Sieg-fried Sassoon and Wilfred Owen as a war poet of distinction and with the popular correspondent Ernie Pyle, whose work he respected and even admired as one of the significant voices of World War II. Today there are those who know nothing else Jarrell wrote but can quote phrases and lines from "The Death of the Ball Turret Gunner."

There are several reasons why Jarrell early in his career was able to achieve easily and, it seemed, almost naturally a place of distinction in contemporary American letters. First of all, he was gifted both with extraordinarily keen powers of observation and with a poet's compulsion to understand his world by making intelligible wholes out of the diverse materials that experience gave him. Thus in imagination he literally went to war and there enjoyed a richer and more varied set of experiences than many who flew the planes, traveled to Europe or the Pacific, participated in combat, and saw the dying. Second, he had a set of sensibilities finely tuned to respond to all orders of living creation—plants, animals wild and domestic, men, women, and children; and for all these he had compassion, disdaining nothing and respecting everything, even though doing so meant being quite out of fashion for one reason or another throughout most of his life. Almost from the beginning, it seems, he was doomed to understand loneliness and the fear that comes with loneliness; early in life he also came to understand what it means to grieve and, having grieved, to experience the slow death of grief. Thus although restricted to the relatively monotonous routine of stateside bases, he learned by training men who would fight what it was like to fight; he read avidly everything he could find about the war he was never to go to; and he talked with returning flyers who bore in their minds and on their bodies the marks of their experiences and who had stories to tell. The result of these experiences was a collection of compositions, successful in varying degrees as poems but almost always interesting and often valuable as records of recurring situations, moods, and attitudes that, like Glückel of Hameln's memoirs, provide something of the living, tangible body of the time. The war years certainly had moments of tedium for Jarrell; undoubtedly at times they were painful. Nevertheless, throughout the wearisome days and months he was able to maintain his equanimity and sense of humor by repeatedly responding to uncongenial situations with surges of creative power that made his existence tolerable, sometimes exciting, and on occasion almost joyous.

For *Selected Poems* he arranged the poems that the war had produced in seven groups, making the whole suggest a survey of the various aspects of the conflict in Europe, in the Pacific theaters, and at home. The subtitles of these groups are "Bombers,"

THE EARLIER POEMS

"The Carriers," "Prisoners," "Camps and Fields," "The Trades" (meaning apparently both trade winds, hence the Pacific, and mercantile exchange),[13] "Children and Civilians," and "Soldiers." The first of these begins with a carefully structured poem from *Losses*, "Eighth Air Force," which consists of four five-line stanzas with rhyming on "man—can" in lines 2, 4, and 5 of all but the second of these, which has the rhymes "one— one—done." One effect of this device, unusual for Jarrell, is to suggest that the principal function of the men, actually boys, viewed here on the evening before a mission is simply that of effective instruments and the nature of their moment of rest, a countdown to further deployment. The speaker, himself a survivor of bombing missions, contemplates the men as they play cards, shave, play with a stray puppy, and perhaps dread the mission to come. He reflects that, for all their appearance of innocence, these men are murderers; yet as Pilate-poet, presenting them to the world, he cannot condemn them ("I find no fault in this just man"), noting that all wash their hands in blood and all are fully involved in whatever guilt is theirs.

The speaker in the poem "Losses" is a dead airman, who confronts another fact of war that officialdom prefers to deal with abstractly: the fact of dying. In periods of training, the speaker tells us, young flyers came to accept dying as incidental to their new occupation. Now overseas they simply continue their training games, never seeing the cities of people that have died in their raids or their fellow airmen who lie dead in the cities they have helped to kill. On the night that he himself died, however, he dreamed the reality of death, knew it for the first time, and imagined the cities asking pathetically for some account of the meaning of the young men's casual game.

By contrast, the dead speaker in "The Death of the Ball Turret Gunner" is one who found life rather than death in the game he was playing. This five-line poem, held tightly together with a rhyme at the end of the second and fifth lines, moves to the nub of its meaning in lines 4 and 5: "loosed from its dream of life,/ I woke. "Before that moment he had slept, first in his mother's womb and then in the state's. Immediately after his brief moment of epiphany, he was reduced by enemy gunfire to the status of a mistake to be washed out of the turret with a steam hose. The disturbing thing about his poem, perhaps the thing that has made it unforgettable for most readers, is not the callousness of the impersonal act reported in the concluding line, but the sudden wasting of that greatest of rarities, a human life lifted to the level of awareness. War is condemned here, to be sure; but, more important, so is the senseless life of most people in a state at peace.

"Transient Barracks" presents an aroused sensibility that has not been so abruptly cut off. Attention here is directed to a typical evening scene in a barracks on an American air base. The barracks is "transient" in the sense that it is one where the men await transfer to more active duty somewhere else. It is transient in reverse for an older flyer shaving himself in the steamy latrine. He has returned, alive and real, to the point where, still unawakened, he began his setting forth to situations that might well have delivered him to the fate of the ball turret gunner. Now the barracks is solid, a place to come to, a place to be. It is real in a sense that the man playing the ocarina, or the soldier looking for something in his barracks bag, or the men lounging in the game room beyond can hardly begin to understand. The man shaving considers himself lucky to have fallen "into the State" awake and without dying.

The speaker in "Siegfried" is also a gunner returned, this time all the way back from bombing raids on Japan to his hometown; his meditation, reported through an effaced narrator, covers most of the range of the preceding four poems. The title calls to mind Wagner's Siegfried, the Germanic hero who inadvertently tasted the blood of the giant-turned-dragon and thereby gained the knowledge which led him ultimately to his tragedy and the tragedy of all his race. In the first section of the poem the gunner does his assigned job precisely as he has been taught to do it. One half of him watches the other half "guiltily," for his business is the same as that of the "murderers" in "Eighth Air

Force"; but the half that mans the weapon feels and understands nothing of the sort and therefore enjoys something like innocence. The guilty half of the man finds a modicum of comfort, however, in a dream of reality that hitherto has sustained him: "It happens as it does because it does." In the second section the bombs have fallen, and the defending fighters have been scattered; yet the Siegfried inside the glass turret still resists involvement, wishing only to return to what he was before the long passage to confrontation with the enemy began. In the third section the hero has returned home to find it changed somewhat—but no matter. He is lucky to have had his wish, or almost had his wish. The change in him is the loss of a leg caused by a shell that penetrated his bubble and exploded; yet for that too he tries to find comfort in his old dream, "It happens as it does because it does." In the final section, however, the dream becomes reality. The blood he tasted—in the air over Japan and in the operating room—was his own. The indifference he had assumed up to that point was his heritage from an insensitive world, and that heritage now encourages him to pretend that the sacrifice he made, not merely in lost flesh but in surrendered spirit, was never a sacrifice at all. Everything happened as it did simply because it did; and to the townspeople of his home, as to his superiors in the war, he has been useful only as a cartridge is useful, and as dispensable.

THE EARLIER POEMS

Jarrell's criticism of the military establishment in which he served during the war, and served well, occupies a fair share of his published letters from that period, but ultimately his dissatisfaction was not with military establishments or even with war. The story of Siegfried is of the hero's progress to a death that reveals the inadequacy of all humanity's goals and its failure to achieve self-knowledge and let its real nature be. Jarrell too had tasted the dragon's blood and thus like Siegfried had begun to have communication with the nature of which he was a part. Thus the tragedy of the woman he depicts in "Burning the Letters" is not that she has suffered the loss of a husband but that she has never known or accepted the life of which death is a necessary component. The first lines of the poem reveal her preoccupation with the notion that the dead pilot preserved in her mind has been trapped in time, as it were, and not allowed to pass into darkness with the destroyed carrier and planes and the weighted corpses. For some years her Christianity with its dying Savior and its life-giving sacrament has offered hope of a triumph over death, but she sees now that the death of her husband, which she never accepted, has also cut her off from the acceptance of death and so from life as well. The absoluteness of the death of Jesus may occur to her fleetingly here as the words "it is finished" pass through her mind; but the final section of the poem suggests that she has at last chosen life in its fullness, which for her involves acknowledging the charred body in its shroud, burning the letters by which she has preserved him in a spurious life, and committing both body and letters along with herself to "the unliving universe in which all life is lost."

The other poems in the section "Carriers" are interesting but thin by comparison with the riches of "Burning the Letters." One reason for their thinness is that they had no auxiliary anchor in Jarrell's own experience. Two of them, "A Pilot from the Carrier" and "Pilots, Man Your Planes," deal with the double jeopardy that haunted navy flyers; that is, the possibility that eventually in some encounter they would lose both plane and carrier. "The Dead Wingman" deals with a situation that they dreaded almost as much: they would lose their companion and be forced to return without knowing what had happened to him. In poems like these the authenticity of the physical circumstances is the essential safeguard against sentimentality, and Jarrell did something like venturing out on a tightrope in attempting them. Even so, he managed in the end to keep his balance, and the less successful performances suffer only slightly by comparison with the masterful half dozen in their own division and the masterpieces in part 1.

The section called "Prisoners" contains poems that critics have praised but no poems that attempt so much so successfully as "Burning the Letters" or "Eighth Air Force." Several kinds of prisoners are pre-

THE EARLIER POEMS

sented. In "Stalag Luft" an American airman in a German prison camp escapes temporarily by dreaming of lying in the grass as a boy with his pet rabbit, pretending that he has been captured by Indians, who marvel at his fortitude. The Jews in "Jews at Haifa" are still prisoners because the ship that presumably was carrying them to freedom has been denied permission to dock at its destination in Palestine; they must return therefore to Cyprus, where they will continue to be prisoners. This should be the end of the world for them, but they refuse to abandon all hope. The three in "O My Name It Is Sam Hall" are American military prisoners in an American prison camp, where they are more bored than desperate. The title of the poem is the title of a song of defiance that their guard suddenly begins to sing, much to their astonishment and amusement. The German prisoners in the poem "Prisoners" are both bored and desperate. They alternately watch the guards that have been assigned to them and the soldiers in the adjacent fields being trained for combat, and they have no communion with either. The speaker observes sentimentally that all three groups are in training for the new world that is to come. The speaker for a fifth group, however, has more legitimate reasons for outrage: many of the prisoners in "A Camp in the Prussion Forest," a concentration camp just liberated by the Allies, are dead bodies stacked for disposal. Victims of the Ultimate Solution, these unfortunates have found in the earth that will bury them the first asylum open to Jews. Like "Jews at Haifa" this poem is a relatively straightforward piece, noteworthy for its intensity and for its eloquent expression of an anger which few readers will hesitate to share.

The section "Camps and Fields" presents memorable glimpses of the soldier's life. The first poem, "A Lullaby," gives a quick succession of such glimpses— sleeping "with seven men within six feet," policing the grounds, cleaning trays after a meal, enduring the indignities of "boot" haircuts and verbal abuse—and pronounces these irritations the mottling that stains "the lying amber of the histories." Presumably Jarrell sees himself here as providing for the story of military life in World War II a corrective like the one Glückel of Hameln provided for the eighteenth century. In "A Front," "The Sick Nought," "Leave," and "The Range in the Desert" he gives additional details, though here they are often suggestive of the particular bases where Jarrell served. "Mail Call" provides a moving generalization: the soldier in that poem, for all his yearning for letters, is lost in the anonymity that his situation imposes and, like most soldiers, wants most of all to hear the reassuring mention of his own name. In "Absent with Official Leave" the same lonely soldier takes leave simply by going to bed and re-creating in his dream a reassuring montage of glimpses of civilian life. In "Second Air Force" he entertains his mother, come to visit her son at the base. Here the reader's

THE EARLIER POEMS

awareness shifts from the soldier to the woman, who is bewildered and a bit intimidated by the world of tar-paper buildings, sand, and Flying Fortresses on the ground and in the air. In the evening she watches the lights of the planes flying overhead, hears the conversation between bomber and fighter, and in her imagination sees the reality that is ahead for such bombers and fighters. "The years meant *this*?" she asks fearfully; but the narrator intervenes to say that for the flyers the bombers are answer enough.

"The Trades" is another group of poems in which Jarrell reaches through his imagination to experiences that he has not known at first hand. The most daring of the lot is "The Rising Sun," in which he re-creates the world of the Japanese soldier from his childhood to the ritual observances at his death. His data are for the most part symbols of Japanese life recognizable to westerners: a woman's "terraces of hair," the wooden pillow she sleeps on, the kite shaped like a carp, the six-cornered roof, dwarfed trees in pots, the threat of earthquake, the warrior tradition, and Shinto with both graciousness and violence in its embrace. The voice in the poem recognizes a contradiction inherent in Japanese life thus presented and pities the child who will be swept from his life of beauty and order into the violence that is his birthright as a man; but it recognizes, too, that war is a deliverer as well as a destroyer and invites those who mourn to participate in the rite

UNDERSTANDING RANDALL JARRELL

that symbolizes communion with this "weak" but liberated ghost.

Most of the other poems in this group deal in one way or another with the Pacific and with the disease of western trade, which, in Jarrell's view, had resulted in the bitter transformation of the region and the conflict that was raging from one end of it to the other. In "A Ward in the States" he presents a group of malaria victims who, though returned home for hospitalization and treatment, are nevertheless prisoners of their original enterprise in that they deliriously imagine themselves still in the tropics. A Negro soldier in "New Georgia" still smarts from the sting of ancient servitude but, feeling that he has done his share of the killing for the world that sent him to war, ironically declares himself free. In "The Dead in Melanesia" the invaders, Japanese and American alike, encounter in the attitude of the natives toward them the relics of an ancient eastern slave trade; the Americans especially, because as inglorious recruits from midwestern cities they are not essentially different from the missionaries who, in the view of the black Melanesians, must have come to them by way of compensation for the dead natives that traders in quest of "niggers" had once left behind. "The Wide Prospect" expands the scene to include both West and East, all engulfed in the conflagration of atomic fire that climaxes the distortions of human life greed and trade have brought about. "All

THE EARLIER POEMS

die for all," the poem concludes, in these years when man at last turns to feeding upon man and makes the bare lives of other men "His last commodity." Finally, in a rhetorically powerful poem entitled "1945: The Death of the Gods," the speaker looks forward to the end of the war of wars, when the man-made deities, the states that men live and die for, have brought themselves to the brink of destruction; and he asks angrily, "Must you learn from your makers how to die?"

The six poems in the group "Children and Civilians" are for the most part accessible to the general reader and need no elaborate explication. One especially, however, will repay careful study. This is an impressive piece entitled "The Angels at Hamburg," in which Jarrell depicts the war as a judgment on trade-obsessed, Protestant North European man. Disillusioned with his centuries-old attempt to adjudicate human behavior in terms of his ideas of good and evil, the knowledge he thought he had gained, he is now unable to grasp the knowledge that angels intuit: for mankind there is no justice on earth, only death. Thus he watches as death dissolves everything he values—soldiers, children, animals, the city itself, day and night—and rests in the judgment of the grave, which he does not comprehend. In a second, much simpler poem about civilians, "The Metamorphoses," a worker, perhaps also from Hamburg, rejoices to see his waterfront flourish with war-generated activity and then

UNDERSTANDING RANDALL JARRELL

lies "all tarry and swollen" in the water of a bombed-out harbor. In this piece the metamorphoses, or change, is, as in "The Angels at Hamburg," from life to death; but here, even though it is the worker who speaks, there is no reaching for comprehensive knowledge. The man is virtually identical with his city, knowing only that on one day he flourished, the next he lay dead amidst the destruction.

The four poems about children are pathetic exemplifications of the same theme. The child in "The State" is insane, having lost mother, sister, and pet cat. The child who beckons the reader to his graveside in "Come to the Stone" asks the same question as the cities in "Losses": Why did I die? And the dead children in "Protocols," victims of extermination camps, grimly compare notes about the method of their going. In "Truth," however, Jarrell concludes the group on a more positive note. The narrator is a London child, who was first told that his father, dead in a bombing raid, had gone to Scotland. Then his sister was dead, and his pet dog Stalky; and he failed to comprehend the death of these also. Removed to a country retreat for displaced children, he is allowed to persist in his incomprehension until one day his mother on a visit brings him a toy dog but says she does not know the dog's name. At this point the boy penetrates the deception kindness has fostered and vigorously repudiates his mother out of hand. The crisis forces her

THE EARLIER POEMS

to acknowledge the fact of death that she has tried to spare him; with that he can at last be reconciled with her, and the two weep together, for the first time in their lives fully parent and child. Unlike the other five poems in the group, this one celebrates a triumph over the despair that war produces; for here the acceptance of death as simple annihilation brings a release in two beings that enables love to flourish between them. For the reader it makes visible a ray of hopefulness that lurks behind the clouds of even the darkest of Jarrell's earlier poems.

Hopefulness also concludes the last group in *Selected Poems*, entitled simply "Soldiers." The first six poems, however, present images that are prevailingly negative. "Port of Embarkation" calls to mind the folly of the abstract ideals men try to live by—truth, reason, and justice—and the reality of blood and death. "The Lines" uses the omnipresent lining up to focus on the dehumanization that occurs in even the simplest exchanges in army existence and on human beings' resistance to it. "A Field Hospital" looks for a pleasant experience and finds it only in the shot of morphine that brings release from a night of pain. In the prose poem "1914" the speaker scans a book, presumably German, of pictures from World War I. The last picture that he describes is that of a dead soldier "half-lying against what seems a hillside," and underneath it is the caption, "Es war ein Traum." (It was a dream). He comments wryly that this is the dream from which no one wakes. The dead soldier in "The Gunner," who gave up his wife and his cat to go off to die, is awake only as the dead in satirical poems are awake; and like the dead cities and the dead children in previous poems he is puzzled by the apparent pointlessness of the action he has completed. Jarrell characteristically has him wonder now whether the cat may not get his medals and his wife receive her pension in mice. "Good-bye, Wendover; Goody-bye, Mountain Home" is a dramatic presentation of the trauma that accompanies the final, absolute separation from one life, the civilian life that has continued with modifications even through the period of army training (wives and children, for example, have been able to live near the base) and the beginning of another. Now comes the transfer to an overseas replacement depot, the departure of loved ones, the shots for exotic diseases like cholera and yellow fever, the precipitous departure for strange places. This is the great crisis in soldiers' lives, but it is a moment of no great importance as the world goes and, he notes, one of which formal history takes no account.

The last three poems in the group, one from *The Seven-League Crutches* and the others never before published, serve as a partial contradiction of the denials of significance that have been made in the preceding six. One of the new pieces, a four-line witticism

THE EARLIER POEMS

entitled "A War," reverses a familiar saying to declare, "You can't break eggs without making an omelette." That is, you can't have disrupted all these lives without accomplishing something. Another new poem, "The Survivor among Graves," expresses the same hope more eloquently, The speaker, a survivor of the war, stands in a military cemetery, looking first at the world beyond with its comfortable habits, values, and religious assurances and then at the graves with their names, numbers, crosses, and a polished granite monument that reads, "These died that we might live." He wonders what life these dead have bought for the living, beyond a few more years of slowly dying. The answer, which the speaker approaches by emotional rather than rational steps, is a "soundless supplication" which the living and the dead share: a cry for reassurance by something, somewhere, that life is more than it seems to be.

The final poem in the section, and thus the final one in *Selected Poems*, is even more positive. This is a dramatic monologue called "Terms," in which a disabled veteran contemplates the steady diminution of life and limb that characterizes his days. He wryly recalls a dream from the night before in which his wooden arm and leg served to make a cross over a grave that seemed to be empty, so that for a moment he fancied he had experienced resurrection. His euphoria gives way to a soberer reflection: "I am my own grave"; and so he wakes. Nevertheless, by daylight he sees a tangible world before him, including a tangible good arm and a tangible wooden one, and with Cartesian reassurance he manages to whisper, "I am a man."

Selected Poems, the collection that Jarrell put together from his first four volumes of verse, is a remarkable achievement in its own right, but it also provides the base upon which his subsequent achievements in poetry rest. *Selected Poems* presents the early experiments in prosody, the gradual settling on a succession of iambics as the prevailing medium for the monologues, dramatic or otherwise, that Jarrell was most inclined to write, and his exploration of a variety of subjects and themes. Here he demonstrates that the field which fascinated him most was the human psyche, and in his early explorations of that field he shows that he had anticipated by several years the popular discovery of its androgynous nature. As was true of most people of Jarrell's generation the global war of 1939–45 had shaped his passage from adolescence to maturity, and something less than half of the poems that he wrote during those years constituted for him a sort of *bildungsroman*, or account of his own apprenticeship. After the war he needed to put formative years behind him and move ahead. This is the justification, if one was needed, for the second half

THE EARLIER POEMS

of the collection, in which he lets the war poems stand in isolation and show clearly what they are: a gifted poet's personal response to challenges, even now still largely unanswered, that threatened for a time to destroy the world he had inherited. The poems of his later years, particularly those in *The Woman at the Washington Zoo* and *The Lost World*, move ahead with the inquiries that had dominated the first half of *Selected Poems*, but now with a strong sense of the paradox at the core of human nature that might never have come to him had he not lived, at least vicariously, through some of the mortal encounters of the Second World War.

Notes

1. *Complete Poems* reprints *Selected Poems*, published by Knopf in 1955. It also reprints without change *The Woman at the Washington Zoo* (1960) and *The Lost World* (1965). In addition it includes seven new poems that Jarrell had finished before his death, all the poems from the first four volumes that had been left out of *Selected Poems*, forty-one published but uncollected poems, and a miscellany of forty-five unpublished pieces.

2. Useful general studies, which will be referred to frequently in this and subsequent chapters, are Suzanne Ferguson, *The Poetry of Randall Jarrell* (Baton Rouge: Louisiana State University Press, 1971); M. Bernetta Quinn, *The Matamorphic Tradition in Modern Poetry*, 2nd ed. (New York: Gordian Press, 1966) and *Randall Jarrell* (Boston: Twayne, 1981), and Charlotte Beck, *Worlds and Lives: The Poetry of Randall Jarrell* (Port Washington, NY: Associated Faculty Press, 1983).

3. Like much of Jarrell's poetry this piece is rich in allusions; but as Jarrell himself says in his introductory note, one can understand the poem without recognizing any of them. Readers who would like additional help in this matter should consult Ferguson 140–42.

4. This is noted by Ferguson 89.

5. Quinn, *Matamorphic Tradition* 186–88, gives a useful analysis of "The Black Swan."

6. Ferguson 127–31 has a good discussion of this poem with special attention to its Freudian implications.

7. Quinn, *Metamorphic Tradition* 172; Ferguson 119–21.

8. John Crowe Ransom, "The Rugged Way of Genius," *Randall Jarrell, 1914–1965,* ed. Robert Lowell, Peter Taylor, and Robert Penn Warren (New York: Farrar, Straus, 1967) 171.

9. Ferguson 103–09 goes through the poem interpreting the succession of figures and allusions that presumably define its action, but no single reading of the accumulation of ambiguities in the poem is ever likely to be entirely satisfactory.

10. Two useful discussions of the poem are Quinn, *Metamorphic Tradition* 174–81, and Beck 80–82.

11. This poem was written at a time when the postman brought mail to the door eleven times each week, twice a day Monday through Friday and once on Saturday.

12. See Jarrell's remarks on Corbière in a review reprinted in *Poetry and the Age* (New York: Knopf, 1953) 158–63.

13. For a discussion of the theme of trade as it appears in Jarrell's *Losses,* see Ferguson 73–89.

CHAPTER THREE

Jarrell as Critic and Essayist

During his lifetime Randall Jarrell published two books of essays and made a list of items to be included in a third. The first of these, *Poetry and the Age* (1953), established him as something more than a brilliant reviewer, and this is the collection by which Jarrell's stature as literary critic has been judged ever since. *A Sad Heart at the Supermarket*, which came out in 1962, is a collection of personal essays that ranges more widely, including one on the stories of Kipling; one on short stories generally; an enthusiastic account of the poetry of Eleanor Taylor, wife of his friend Peter Taylor; a review of André Malraux's *The Voices of Silence*; and an explanation of how he wrote "The Woman at the Washington Zoo." Other essays deal more or less directly with the decline of taste in mid-twentieth-century America. *The Third Book of Criticism* appeared four years after his death, in 1969, and contained two early and (and uneven) pieces on Auden; the introductions to his anthology *Six Russian*

Short Novels and his collection of Kipling's English short stories; essays on Wallace Stevens, Robert Graves, Christina Stead's *The Man Who Loved Children* (a novel Jarrell championed enthusiastically for two decades), and Frost's "Home Burial"; and a lecture, "Fifty Years of American Poetry," that he delivered at the National Poetry Festival in Washington in 1962. A fourth volume, entitled *Kipling, Auden & Co.: Essays and Reviews* (1980) made available virtually all of Jarrell's uncollected criticism, much of it first published in *The Nation, The New Republic, Vogue, The Partisan Review, The Yale Review,* and *The New York Times Book Review.* In addition, the volume reprinted five essays from *A Sad Heart at the Supermarket* (by that time out of print) and the essay on Kipling's English stories from *The Third Book of Criticism* ("so as to gather all of Jarrell's criticism of Kipling between the covers of one book").

Persons familiar with the work of Jarrell the reviewer, particularly the early Jarrell, though they admired his unflagging perceptiveness and his wit, admit to having winced frequently at the vitriol he seemed prepared to throw at almost anyone who asked the reader to give attention to work that was careless, professionally irresponsible, or untouched by genius. These older readers probably did not need to be reminded of what some of the early Jarrell reviews were like, and one suspects that the mature Jarrell would

JARRELL AS CRITIC AND ESSAYIST

never have gone out of his way to make accessible much of the material that this last volume dropped so casually on the younger generation's bedside table. Even so, nothing in it diminishes Jarrell's stature as critic, and his judgments from the beginning had a significant effect on the taste of the American reading public—and perhaps an effect on the direction of letters in postwar America as well.

Jarrell's first essay for *The Southern Review* (Autumn, 1935), written when he was twenty-one, is a good example. It is an omnibus review of ten new works of fiction by a group of writers that included Ellen Glasgow, Erskine Caldwell, Stark Young, Willa Cather, and Rachel Field. Jarrell's judgments are remarkably consistent with those that prevail after fifty years of reflection and sifting. He found Glasgow's style and perceptions commonplace but not without occasional moments of power. He obviously admired Caldwell as a craftsman but found him sentimental in his undiscriminating use of brutality. Just as obviously, he did not care for Stark Young: "Sometimes . . . snobblish, sometimes sentimental, sometimes he shows a disquieting admiration for moral perceptions or stylistic effects which do not seem to the reader admirable at all." His four paragraphs on Willa Cather's *Lucy Gayheart* combine qualified praise for an unpretentious novel with a clear perception of the qualities that have kept Cather's work alive for more than half

UNDERSTANDING RANDALL JARRELL

a century. Rachel Field was highly thought of by other critics at the time, but Jarrell summarized his opinion of *Time Out of Mind* with the observation that on a certain level it "is quite a good story; but this level is surprisingly low."

Understandably readers came in time to look for quips and cutting remarks in Jarrell's reviews, and sensitive authors came to fear them. He called Frederic Prokosch "a decerebrate Auden, an Auden popularized for mass consumption." He published a devastating essay on Archibald MacLeish's *The Fall of the City* in *The Sewanee Review* (Spring, 1943), in which he called it, among a great many other things, a "black-and-white political cartoon, plainly at variance with most of the facts." Irritated with Conrad Aiken's fluency and lack of substance, he wrote in *The New Republic* (February 17, 1941) that Aiken "seems as much at ease as Merlin pulling a quarter out of a schoolboy's nose." In time Jarrell came to regret some of his flippancies. Approaching his middle years he said that he had come to understand pain of the spirit and was increasingly reluctant to take pleasure in inflicting it, however justified the pain might be. Still, his honesty tended to redeem even the more outrageous sallies of his rambunctious youth. Painful or not, his judgments more often than not turned out to be right, and he made them all out of a deep concern for literary values. His reputation as a critic has, if anything, been enhanced by the republication of his more ephemeral pieces.

JARRELL AS CRITIC AND ESSAYIST

Jarrell's earliest essays also give evidence of an intellect that was flexible as well as formidable, one that he might have deployed successfully in any number of directions; but being congenitally disinclined to be a follower, he eschewed the route of apprenticeship and insisted from the outset on finding a direction that would allow him to be uniquely himself. He managed to maintain his indifference to the interests of some of his Fugitive mentors in the tradition of the American south and to their subsequent flirtation with agrarianism. He resisted attempts to make him set down his principles and thus came close to annoying James Laughlin of New Directions, who wanted a preface for the group of poems Jarrell contributed to *Five Young American Poets* (1940).[1] And he gave evasive answers to the series of questions posed by John Ciardi, who had included him in the anthology *Mid-Century American Poets* (1950).[2] Subsequently, in almost a quarter of a century of writing about literature, he never produced aesthetic statements or rationales comparable to those in Warren's "Pure and Impure Poetry" or the essays in Ransom's *The World's Body* or Tate's several volumes of criticism.

The closest he ever came to producing a set of principles was in "The Age of Criticism," the fourth essay in his first collection, *Poetry and the Age*. There he endorsed the commonplace that the present age is one of criticism and explained that this is so because most people can no longer read. The deficiency is just as conspicuous in university professors and scholars, he said, as it is among the general public. The latter read less because their leisure is increasingly filled with other occupations; the professors read less because they feel compelled to spend their time strengthening their specialties by reading books and articles *about* literature rather than literature itself. Hence the need for the critic, who properly is nothing more than a loving, self-effacing reader who seeks only to lead others to the monument and then disappear in the presence of the thing itself. If all of us were the readers we ought to be, he said, there would be no need for criticism.

Jarrell's own practice as critic was always just this and nothing more: to bring his readers to the monument and entice them, cajole them if need be, into seeing for themselves. Usually his strategy, whether writing reviews for *The Nation* or producing essays for *The Kenyon Review,* was to make a series of affirmations, punctuated by occasional quips (sometimes characterized by detractors as wisecracks), followed by a list, occasionally divided into best and second best, of the pieces under consideration that he preferred. In short reviews, poetry chronicles, and surveys like the one he delivered at the National Poetry Festival in Washington in 1962 he usually limited himself to judgments and quips; but in all of his critical writing he seemed to be implying that the work of the

JARRELL AS CRITIC AND ESSAYIST

critic was an activity best summed up in a remark he made in 1959: "Art is long, and critics are the insects of a day."[3] During his lifetime more formal critics dismissed this procedure of Jarrell's as simplistic. Hindsight has compelled acknowledgment from both critics and general readers that many of the affirmations still stand as defensible critical perceptions, that the quips continue to charm as wit, and that the lists still serve admirably as guides to what is most characteristic of the subject's work.

For Jarrell criticism was, like his poetry and his fiction, simply one more extension of his person—normally an ephemeral extension, to be sure (like the song of an insect), but dignified in his case by the fact that he was himself a poet and a writer of fiction. In conversation the word he most often used to indicate his reason for a particular judgment was *taste*. It was taste, he said, that told him that a piece of clothing was or was not appropriate, that a musical selection was good (though he knew music mainly from records), and that one painting was preferable to another. He recognized the implication that his reliance on taste had for some. "Using such a word as *taste*," he wrote in "Poets, Critics, and Readers," "helps to make us believe that there is some passive faculty that responds to the new work of art, registering the work's success or failure."[4] *Passive* is the key word here. The faculty was real enough, he thought, but it was not some kind of aesthetic litmus, and it was not widely disseminated. In the same essay he went on to say that "the new work must call forth in us an active power analogous to that which created it." Here he was confident of his ground, for Jarrell believed in nothing if not his own gift of creativity. He might just as easily have been a painter, a composer, or a fashion designer, he felt; but by accident of circumstances he was a poet, and the creativity that had made him a poet, he was sure, qualified him to be a critic of other forms of art as well—a critic and an interpreter.

As a critic of writing Jarrell felt especially free to promote his personal enthusiasms, sometimes without very much explanation. Among the writers he praised virtually without qualification were Eleanor Taylor, Adrienne Rich, Cristina Stead (though mainly for one novel), Elizabeth Bishop, Katherine Hoskins, and Robert Graves. He also felt free—indeed obligated—to point out the shortcomings in certain established writers whose accomplishments might have been expected to intimidate a relatively young critic like himself, among them T. S. Eliot, Ezra Pound, his old friends and mentors Allen Tate and Robert Penn Warren, and his closest friend (aside from Peter Taylor) among contemporaries, Robert Lowell. Moreover, though he began and ended an ardent admirer of the poetry of W. H. Auden, he did not hesitate throughout his life to call the older poet to task for a variety of literary sins, including sentimentality, vagueness, and banality.

He could also recommend to public attention and admiration older authors who he felt had been neglected by fashionable writers and literary critics. The best example here is Walt Whitman, who in an age of Eliot, Pound and such journals as *The Southern Review* and *Scrutiny* had suffered the fate of being taken for granted.[5] Jarrell began by wittily postulating a war (not entirely imaginary) in which the partisans of Henry James were waging a life-and-death battle with the partisans of Whitman, and then he reflected that James had once given Edith Wharton a private reading of Whitman that left them both "shaken and silent." The source of Whitman's greatness, Jarrell insisted, lies, as greatness always does, in the "minute particulars" of the poetry, not in some nebulous cumulative excellence. "All the dead lines in the world," he observed, "will not make one live poem"; then he added that with Whitman's poetry one does not need to explain or argue this point but merely to quote. After that he proceeded to give a demonstration.

This took the form of a three-page mosaic, set in a single paragraph, of metaphors, epithets, and concrete detail, all illustrative of Whitman's lifelong preoccupation with things both static and active: men, women, children, plants, animals, insects, weather phenomena of various kinds, and such artifacts as scythes, drainpipes, and kitchen utensils, all set forth in nouns, active verbs, and (used sparingly) precise adjectives. Then dismissing some insensitive reader's inclination to detect a resemblance here to Thomas Wolfe (a writer much admired during Jarrell's formative years, though never by Jarrell), he pronounced Whitman even at his worst "ingeniously bad" and went on to say, "Only a man with the most extraordinary feel for language, or none whatsoever, could have cooked up Whitman's worst messes." To substantiate his points further he provided several pages of extended quotation interspersed with brief comments suggesting possible comparisons with Berlioz; James at his best; Chekhov; and Tennyson ("the most skillful of all Whitman's contemporaries"), who suffered from the limitation imposed by the forms he used, a limitation Whitman happily was able to avoid.

As for Whitman's notorious contradictions, which Whitman himself acknowledged and airily accepted, Jarrell saw these as inherent in the comprehensive view of the world that was the supreme gift Whitman passed on to his readers. He admitted that Whitman did not give us "the controlled . . . contradictions of the great lyric poets," but he pointed out that Whitman should not be compared with the lyric poets at all but with Homer or the writers of the sagas or perhaps the Melville who wrote *Moby-Dick*.

JARRELL AS CRITIC AND ESSAYIST

Where the qualities of a Walt Whitman are concerned, he wrote, the critic can only point "in despair and wonder" and call them by their names.

This is a good example of Jarrell the critic "coming clean," exposing the critic's pretensions, acknowledging the limitations of his role; for he firmly believed that in the end the critic when dealing with works that are truly great or that have a touch of greatness—Homer's, Shakespeare,'s, Goethe's, or Whitman's—can only stare in wonder and point out his discoveries to others. Being modest (or perhaps innocent as well), he did not say here (though he had elsewhere implied as much in his remarks about taste) that the critic who would write in this way and expect to be effective must have eyes and ears and imagination comparable to the eyes and ears and imagination that had produced the works under inspection. In one way, however, Jarrell failed to measure up to his own prescription: try as he would, he could not be self-effacing. His better critical essays almost inadvertently create the impression of classrooms with Jarrell presiding as teacher, exhorting, reassuring, explaining where necessary, occasionally indulging in witticisms. For those who expect their critics to maintain objectivity, with at least an illusion of distance, this can be disconcerting; but most agree that the dividends in illumination and insight more than compensate for indulging Jarrell in this regard.

Another neglected writer whom he helped to return to prominence was Rudyard Kipling. The project came about almost by accident when Doubleday asked him to select fifty of Kipling's stories for an anthology to be published under their Hanover House imprint. Jarrell's introductory essay, "On Preparing to Read Kipling," subsequently found its way into *A Sad Heart at the Supermarket* and after that into *Kipling, Auden & Co.* as well. In the last collection it was accompanied by two more essays on Kipling that he had written for shorter anthologies in Doubleday's Anchor series. One of these, "In the Vernacular," prefaced a collection of tales about India; the other, "The English in England," prefaced a companion volume of stories about England. Jarrell's interest in Kipling had begun in childhood; it was still strong during his Vanderbilt days, when he once winced to hear his teacher Ransom speak disparagingly of *Plain Tales from the Hills*.[6] He had no illusions about Kipling's limitations and freely admitted that he was no Shakespeare—not even a Turgenev or a Chekhov. Even so, Jarrell pronounced him a great genius, a great neurotic, a great professional, "one of the most skillful writers who have ever existed," and unbeatable when it came to creating his own unique kind of story.

His defense of the man and his work was not unlike the defense he mounted on behalf of Whitman. Once more he began with a citation from Henry

James, who, it turns out, was as appreciative of Kipling as he had been of the American poet. Then he asked readers to divest themselves of everything they had ever heard or believed about the man and take a fresh look for themselves. The Kipling who emerged in the next eight pages or so was a vastly talented reporter who put truth above rhetoric and (like Jarrell himself) produced a body of writing that was an extension of his own person and reflected his response to the specter of a collapsing world of presumably benevolent imperialism. In that vision, which he shared with all enlightened Anglo-Indians, Jarrell said, Kipling had recognized in Victorian England the truth of Thomson's City of Dreadful Night; and that knowledge, which he had tried futilely to communicate in his stories, made him sadly congenial with the debacle of the First World War ("the death and anguish of Europe") that took his own son.

In a sense Jarrell's three principal essays on Robert Frost constitute a rehabilitation of that literary figure also. Jarrell knew Frost fairly well and brought him to Greensboro on several occasions to give readings to the students. The first of these essays, "The Other Frost," included in *Poetry and the Age*, contains sharp criticism of some of Frost's most popular poetry as well as of the man himself; and by comparison with the images that Jarrell presented of Whitman and Kipling, his picture of Frost seems almost diminutive. "A sort of Olympian Will Rogers out of *Tanglewood Tales,*" is only one of several disparaging epithets with which he begins the essay. Nevertheless, "The Other Frost" almost certainly places in focus the Frost that will command the interest and respect of knowledgeable readers in generations to come. This is the Frost of "The Witch of Coos," "A Servant to Servants," "After Apple-Picking," "Directive," "Design," "Provide Provide," and "Home Burial." Jarrell's second essay, also in *Poetry and the Age*, contains excellent readings of several of these poems, including "Provide Provide" and "Directive," which he calls "one of the strangest and most characteristic, most dismaying and most gratifying, poems any poet has even written." A detailed reading of "Home Burial" was reprinted in *The Third Book of Criticism*. Here he called Frost "a complete and representative poet," and by that he meant a poet who had looked at the world and attempted, with remarkable success, to set it forth, all of it, as it appeared to him. Frost's view was inevitably partial, but that was not entirely his fault; it was as comprehensive as Frost was capable of giving, and that was enough to leave most readers in wonder and awe and rejoicing.

Jarrell presents his homage to Wallace Stevens in two essays: "Reflections on Wallace Stevens" in *Poetry and the Age* and "The Collected Poems of Wallace Stevens," which first appeared in *The Yale Review* in

JARRELL AS CRITIC AND ESSAYIST

1955, the year of Stevens's death, and later in *The Third Book of Criticism*. In the first Jarrell spends a good deal of time being witty (for example, he compares *Harmonium* to a travel poster); and he criticizes Stevens for philosophizing too much and avoiding figures of earth, "always swinging between baroque and rococo." Yet even as he criticizes, he pronounces Stevens one of the true poets of our age and concludes, somewhat condescendingly, with what is probably the most quoted sentence in all of his criticism: "A good poet is someone who manages, in a lifetime of standing out in thunderstorms, to be struck by lightning five or six times; a dozen or two dozen times and he is great." From the second essay one concludes that Stevens was more than great. There Jarrell retracts his earlier judgment that Stevens philosophized too much. He declares it a virtue that he wrote steadily with or without inspiration for most of his life, and was able at the end to put into poetry the rich insights that the end of a lifetime brought him. Then characteristically Jarrell provides a list of sixty or so poems, which as he puts it, is sufficient to give a "dazzlingly definite" idea of the things that are exceptional about Stevens's work.

Poetry and the Age contains two essays on Marianne Moore, both in part defenses against critics who persisted in saying that she was not really a poet at all. For Jarrell, as for T. S. Eliot, Moore was one of the finer poets of contemporary America; and he warmed to her work as he had been unable to warm to the austerities of Wallace Stevens. The things he especially admired in Moore's work were her use of particularities; her recognition that relationships are the realities in this world and that everything is related to everything else; her unembarrassed recourse to "expression in general" (that is, common discourse) as opposed to "poetic expression"; and her refusal to consider anything unpoetic or unfit for inclusion in her unpretentious but precise lines. Having said all this in three remarkable pages, Jarrell translates these virtues into a series of comparisons: as tersely conclusive as Grimm, as wise as Goethe, as beguiling as Beatrix Potter, as purely magical as Alban Berg, as elevated as the Old Testament, and as morally and rhetorically magnificent as St. Paul. Near the end of the second essay he clinches his points with the customary list of her best poems—pieces, he says, quoting Moore's own words, that make the reader feel "a life prisoner, but reconciled."

The reader of Jarrell's essay on John Crowe Ransom,[7] his onetime teacher and mentor, may detect behind the appearance of self-confident ease a note of diffidence that is rare in Jarrell's criticism. In the first sentence he says that Ransom's poems are "about everything from Armageddon to a dead hen," as indeed they are, though put thus baldly Ransom's range diminishes to the level of a wisecrack. Near the end he takes note of Ransom's influence on "at least three good poets"—Robert Graves, Allen Tate, and Robert Penn Warren; then he suggests that these were influenced "more by his accident than by his essence" and adds, "To expect Tate's and Warren's poems to be influenced by Ransom's is like expecting two nightmares to be influenced by a daydream." The list of best poems here comes at the middle, and the essay ends with a virtuoso performance that is more Jarrell than Ransom: "a recollected Breugelish landscape of the country of Ransom's poems," in which familiar images of the older man's poetry are recognizable but only as shapes translated into an alien mode. One is tempted to think that Jarrell never quite escaped a youthful intimidation by the confident tone of Ransom's poems (those written after *Poems About God*) and felt uncomfortable at realizing that while he could capture the accidents and even make sport with them, he still could not lay hand on the elusive essence.

He found the work of William Carlos Williams, a poet not attractive to Jarrell's early mentors, considerably more to his liking. Williams is the subject of two of the last essays in *Poetry in the Age*; he receives more than half of the space in a third and shares a fourth with Richard Wilbur and Robert Lowell. In all four Jarrell addresses a sophisticated public that, even as he wrote, was beginning to accord Williams the respect that since then it has more than amply confirmed. For Williams, Jarrell had such epithets as *generous, spontaneous, open, humanitarian, liberal,* and *democratic,* all signifying the qualities by which the young Jarrell had thought himself differentiated and distanced from the austerely formal Fugitives who had ignited but at the same time frustrated his youthful genius. Acknowledging that parts 2 and 3 of *Paterson* were discouraging, he declared part 1 a work of genius, a "microcosm which he has half-discovered, half-invented," narrower than Whitman's but strongly reminiscent of that older poet's world. Jarrell's most telling compliment is probably his suggestion that Williams has an unusual dislike and distrust of Authority (Jarrell's capital), a dislike that aroused sympathies which even the mature Jarrell may never have fully recognized in himself. Mere dislike of authority probably would not have been enough to win his approval; but Williams, in defiance of the "establishment" that had exalted Eliot for more than a generation, managed to produce a body of durable poetry of a radically different kind. He had challenged Goliath without losing either his life or his identity. "If you have gone to the moon in a Fourth of July rocket you built yourself," Jarrell quipped at the conclusion of *Poetry and the Age*, "you can be forgiven for looking askance at Pegasus." He may have been thinking of his own achievement.

JARRELL AS CRITIC AND ESSAYIST

He was almost certainly thinking about his own achievement and career in some of the things he wrote about Auden, the idol of his youth who never ceased to amaze, challenge, and frequently anger him. Writing in *The Yale Review* in 1955 (in one of the essays reprinted in *Kipling, Auden & Co.*) he could speak of the "flatness" of *Nones* and the "comfortable frivolity" of *The Shield of Achilles*; yet in the last sentence he could not forbear recalling nostalgically that in the thirties Auden had produced "some of the strongest, strangest, and most original poetry that anyone has written in this century." Anger triumphs over nostalgia, however, in essays that he wrote for *The Southern Review* in 1941 and for *The Partisan Review* in 1945. These were included in *The Third Book of Criticism* as "Changes of Attitude and Rhetoric in Auden's Poetry," and "Freud to Paul: The Stages of Auden's Ideology." There Jarrell set forth the grounds for his disaffection at length, explaining in the first essay how Auden had abandoned his early preoccupation with the resources of English language in favor of a preoccupation with rhetoric. Thus, whereas in the beginning he had done what poets ought to do—namely, extend creatively the range of the language—midway in his productive career he had let his language go flat and resorted to rhetorical tricks that sometimes startle but never completely obscure the fact that his thought had slipped to a prosaic level commensurate with his diction. Even

for readers who resist the evaluation, Jarrell's analysis
of Auden's style here should be extremely valuable,
particularly his account of the idiosyncratic language
in Auden's early poetry. The results of what must have
been a youthful and loving scrutiny of Auden's work
is set forth in a remarkable list of salient characteristics, twenty-six in all. An alert reader will note that
many of these are characteristics of Jarrell's own ad-
venturous early poetry.

Equally remarkable in the same essay is a list of
elements that went into the "world order" that Jarrell
has Auden making to oppose to the world of "late-
capitalist society in which [during the thirties] he
found himself." These include Marxism, Freudian psychology, fairy tales and folklore, boyish sources of
value (including flying and polar exploration), the
world of the biological sciences, and homosexuality.
Jarrell seems to have had no interest in the last of
these, but he shared fully Auden's interest in the first
four, and he understood Auden's interest in the fifth, it
being at the time, as he said, practically incapable of
being corrupted by capitalist culture. In any case this
was a schema of the Auden Jarrell admired, and one
finds echoes of it throughout his first four volumes of
poetry, where it might almost serve as a schema of the
Jarrell one sees there.

The second essay deals with Auden's shifts in ideology, "from Freud to Paul," and is if anything more

JARRELL AS CRITIC AND ESSAYIST

disapproving than the first one. In Jarrell's view the later Auden ceased to be serious but adopted a pose of solemnity that masked his ingenious maneuvers to avoid confronting enemies far more formidable than capitalism. Jarrell's generation confronted them head-on by going to war; Auden had abandoned a decadent Europe for the relative tranquillity of the United States, where he moved steadily toward the position of St. Paul (as Jarrell presents it), accepting our involvement in original sin and waiting passively to be saved by grace. Ten years later Jarrell was still paying lip service to the poet Auden might have been. "Auden's laundry list would be worth reading," he wrote," and then he added, "I speak as one who's read it many times, all rhymed and metered."[8]

Jarrell wrote on other contemporary poets, of course, but not at great length and not with the intensity that he displayed in writing about the ones that have been discussed here. Near the end of his life, in the fall of 1962, he delivered a lecture at the National Poetry Festival in Washington, "Fifty Years of American Poetry." This was published the following year in *Prairie Schooner,* and it was included as the last item in *The Third Book of Criticism.* This piece is literally a distillation of Jarrell's critical performances of a lifetime enclosed in a single vessel. In it he occasionally paraphrases earlier essays; sometimes he quotes verbatim without indicating that he is serving up older material.[9] No matter: everything seems fresh and perfectly appropriate in its new setting; and from this simple survey the reader can get a better sense of Jarrell's achievement in criticism than from any other single essay that he wrote. His procedure is also a distillation of past procedures; he begins at the beginning and reviews the poets roughly in chronological order, making judgments as he goes, occasionally enlivening the proceedings with a witticism, and providing lists so that the reader can go and confirm the judgments for himself. As always he presents himself as unpretentious teacher and guide, without apology, fully confident of the rightness of his own taste.

His judgments on Frost, Stevens, Ransom, Moore, and Williams remain essentially unchanged. These figures are still the larger stars in his firmament, and the mature Jarrell even enhances the luster of some of them—notably Frost, Stevens, and Ransom—by omitting most of the mildly disparaging qualifications he had recorded earlier. He begins by noticing with respect Edwin Arlington Robinson, Edgar Lee Masters, and Carl Sandburg, praising Robinson for his somber honesty, Masters for his historical truth about nineteenth-century American life, and Sandburg for his innocence. He becomes almost enthusiastic, however, in the page he devotes to Vachel Lindsay, who had the courage, or the eccentricity, to be a poet in a world that had little patience with artists. Lindsay's reward is to be remem-

JARRELL AS CRITIC AND ESSAYIST

bered for having more imagination and more command of his art than most of his contemporaries.

Jarrell devotes three pages to Ezra Pound, whom he recognized as a true critic and a great poet, though one marred by his own obsessions ("a moral and intellectual disaster") and by his choice of a form, *The Cantos*, that permitted him much of the time not to write poetry at all. Yet Pound survives, he notes; for not even the worst in the man and his work or the worst in the age that produced him has been able to destroy *The Cantos* or obscure the beauties, lines, poems, resurrections of the past, that they contain.

Two pages are given to T. S. Eliot, and Jarrell apologizes, after a fashion, for presuming to write on one about whom so much has already been written. At the time of the essay Jarrell had in fact been talking among friends about an essay on Eliot that he planned to do. He never published such an essay, but he let his comments on Eliot in the 1962 survey suggest the direction the essay might have taken. Midway through his remarks he asks, "Won't the future say to us in helpless astonishment: 'But did you actually believe that all those things about objective correlative, classicism, the tradition, apply to *his* poetry'?"[10] Then, speaking for the future with characteristic sureness, he sweeps away all the academic talk and pronounces Eliot "one of the most subjective and daemonic poets who ever lived." Beneath Prufrock, "The Waste Land,"

Murder in the Cathedral, and *The Family Reunion*, he declares, lies a poetry that Eliot's own age, mistaking the personal struggle for a realistic photograph of the time, has never seen. Nevertheless, he concedes, the age has loved the right poet and the right poems, and for that it is entitled to take satisfaction.

E. E. Cummings gets two pages also, but Jarrell does not see him as the poet of the age. Cummings is the circus performer among poets, striving always for the limit of every possibility. Like all intelligent people he recognizes that words describe the world imperfectly at best; consequently he manipulates words in all the ways he can think of and teases his readers into guessing what they might mean. As a rule, however, they have only quasi-denotations in the use he makes of them and hence only vague or contradictory meanings. His poems amuse but do not often enlighten.

After thus dismissing Cummings, Jarrell turns briefly to Conrad Aiken, whom he had offended in an early review. He still allows him only second best in the rankings ("poems that come close to being good poems, without ever quite being so"), compares him to Frederick Delius ("undifferentiating wash of lovely sounds"), and pronounces his work nostalgic verse that "turns everything into itself." He also gives short shrift, but respectful praise, to the work of Allen Tate, Aiken's friend and the early mentor to whom Jarrell had dedicated his first volume of poetry, *Blood for a*

Stranger. Tate's poems lack charm and human
warmth, he says, but he names three of them—"The
Mediterranean" and, somewhat oddly, "Mother and
Son" and "The Cross"—for which the current state of
neglect will "surely be temporary." Two other poets
whom he dismisses with a paragraph of comment are
Robinson Jeffers and Archibald MacLeish; these receive only faint praise.

As he comes closer to the current scene, Jarrell
understandably resorts to broad sweeps, making a list
of poets he would like to write favorably about if there
were "room" and naming four groups of practicing poets for whom he had little use. Howard Nemerov and
his old friends John Berryman and Delmore Schwartz
head the list of the good poets ("interesting and intelligent") followed by fourteen others, about most of
whom he had written favorable reviews at one time or
another. The groups that he disapproved of were the
beatniks (their method of writing precludes their ever
producing poetry); the followers of Yvor Winters
("learned imbecility, a foolishness of the schools"); the
academic, tea-party imitators of Richard Wilbur; and
the writers of "feminine verse" (Edna St. Vincent Mil-
lay, Eleanor Wylie, Leonie Adams, and Louise Bo-
gan), though these occasionally wrote good poems.
He was careful to exclude from the last group his favorite women writers, Marianne Moore, Eleanor Taylor (for whose *Wilderness of Ladies* he had written an

introduction), Adrienne Rich, Katherine Hoskins, and Elizabeth Bishop, whose *Poems* he called "one of the best books an American poet has written."

Of Hart Crane he has somewhat more to say, though he finds *The Bridge* unsuccessful as a unified work of art. Like Cummings, Crane was a manipulator of words, and like Auden he was a master of rhetorical strategies. But Jarrell counterpoises these shortcomings with such imprecise phrases as "magical successes" and "soaring rapture of something unprecedented, absolutely individual"; and he singles out "Black Tambourine," "Repose of Rivers," "National Winter Garden," and "Voyages II" as pieces of special distinction. He gives similar praise to the work of Robert Penn Warren and Theodore Roethke. The work of Warren's that most impresses him is the long poem *Brother to Dragons* with its "traumatic subject" of original sin in a world without a Savior and only raw nature and the shaky grace of custom to fall back on. In contrast, he finds Roethke's great distinction in the short lyric (for example, "My Papa's Waltz" and "I Knew a Woman") but notes that his style is still changing.

In conclusion Jarrell comments on three poets with whom he had often been compared by other reviewers. The first of these is Karl Shapiro, who had recovered quickly and with good grace from drubbings that Jarrell had given him in early reviews. Jarrell takes note of Shapiro's "visual and satiric force," his precision and "memorable exactness of realization," and his honesty. The second poet is Richard Wilbur, whom Jarrell here describes with a wit that rises above mere cleverness, calling him one who "obsessively sees, and shows, the bright underside of every dark thing" and noting his "lyric calling-to-life of the things of this world."

It was inevitable that Jarrell should conclude with a poet who had been his friend from Kenyon days, who had had a notable influence on his own work, and who had reached a level of achievement more remarkable, perhaps, than that of any other contemporary poet: Robert Lowell. Lowell's poetry, Jarrell says at the outset, is the poetry of shock; but crude or magnificent, what shocks us is almost always fact, "the live stumbling block that we fall over and feel to the bone." Moreover, it is always the only fact that Lowell or anyone else can write about truthfully, the fact personally perceived, seen, and felt. In the beginning Lowell sometimes "bullied" his facts, forced them to submit to a preconceived order. In his later work he has allowed facts to lead their own lives, and his poetry accordingly has gone on developing in grandeur and in power.

Jarrell's "Fifty Years of American Poetry" turned out to be the final statement by an observer of remarkable authority and perception. In the histories of formal literary criticism Jarrell will probably occupy at most a modest paragraph or two. As has been noted, he never devised a system to incorporate his insights or articulated a set of principles to explain them. Yet his judgments have already proved to have extraordinary staying power, and the reasons for that are not difficult to understand. He was, first of all, endowed with genius, which for a variety of reasons he chose to deploy in the study and creation of literature. Second, though he recognized that any vision or insight he might have would necessarily be personal, he accepted the integrity of the external world on faith and proceeded on the assumption that he possessed sufficient means at least to touch that world with his senses and perceive its reality. Third, he respected what he saw, heard, and touched, and early in his career decided that anything he might create could at most be a window on the world that he had been gifted by luck or grace to know somewhat better than his fellows. He thought of his poems as such windows, and he thought the same of his fiction and his essays—different devices, but all serving the same objective. And the objective, for Jarrell, was always to know the world and make it known.

It is understandable that Jarrell should have been accused of arrogance throughout most of his life. Being human and therefore limited he saw, as does everyone with partial vision. Hence he was often

JARRELL AS CRITIC AND ESSAYIST

mistaken in his judgments, sometimes in ways that observers with less acute vision saw before he did. Again, being human he sometimes bristled when others challenged him. Nevertheless, Jarrell's basic stance never changed: he loved the world and the creatures in it. He respected the right of all things to be themselves; and as he would not tolerate gladly or for long anyone's attempt to make him submit to authority, so he resisted any move to impose restrictive authority on others, whether by rule or by custom or by art. He lived by the conviction that all things, animate and inanimate, should be freed of inhibitions and left to fulfill their own natures; and for this categorizing historians in time to come may well label him an American romantic. By implication he advocated the same freedom in his own poetry, and he praised other poets, provided they possessed a modicum of genius, in proportion as they freed themselves of the temptation to make displays of virtuosity and simply let their work stand as uninhibited but self-effacing pointers to the world of common experience.

Jarrell's essays did not always deal with literary criticism. *Poetry and the Age* deals exclusively with literary matters, as does *The Third Book of Criticism*; but Jarrell wrote about American culture too, about education, and about art. From time to time he also wrote about music, though he played no instrument and had only a listener's knowledge of it. Readers of

Pictures from an Institution are properly impressed by the authority with which he created a professional musician to serve as one of the central characters of that novel, but this was authority of the kind that enabled a Shakespeare to create credible Macbeths and Cleopatras. Music for Jarrell, like language, was a medium for the exploration of the world of human feelings and perceptions; and the same thing was true of the graphic and plastic arts. In his view the world of things must be the primary object of any artist's attention, his art a secondary concern—as in poetry, a means to know the world and make it known.

He made his point in an essay reprinted in *Kipling, Auden & Co.*, "Against Abstract Expressionism." Painting, he said there, is a kind of metaphor for the reality it stands for. Sometimes the relationship is a rigorously mimetic one, and sometimes it is much less so, but the relationship is always present. Abstract expressionism removes half of the equation, the half that is the world, and so removes from art the necessity of imitation. In Jarrell's view such a development could only be deplored, but no art, he observes optimistically, regardless of its pretensions, will ever be able to hold out against nature indefinitely.

Abstract expressionism as he saw it, was simply one consequence of pursuing to a logical conclusion the American ideal of purity, which derives from a dangerously limited view of human nature and the world, one that in the end could destroy man—or de-

JARRELL AS CRITIC AND ESSAYIST

humanize him—just as readily as the bombs and other war machines that same ideal had created. Throughout his career Jarrell continued to be concerned about this and other things that he considered aberrations of the American spirit, and in some of the early poems his concern took the form of sharp indictments. By the time he came to put together his second collection of essays, *A Sad Heart at the Supermarket*, he had mellowed considerably, and the indictments there were muted with the sadness that the title refers to. The first essay, "The Intellectual in America," serves as a preface to all the others. The specific object of its attack is the disease of anti-intellectualism that swept the United States in the decade and a half following World War II. Anti-intellectualism, as he recognized, was not something new; and it was not a simple malady but a complex disease that even de Tocqueville in the early days of the republic had seen as endemic in the nation. Jarrell was not prepared to offer either an explanation of the problem or a remedy for it, but he could and did continue to provide eloquent laments that its existence was continuing to vitiate American life. Nevertheless, in spite of his strictures Jarrell never ceased to love his country or mankind generally or to nourish the hope that both might somehow see the need to change.

Jarrell's capacity for love is best demonstrated in an essay that he never saw fit to reprint, or perhaps never found an opportunity to do so. This was the piece that he wrote for *The Nation* on Ernie Pyle

shortly after that popular correspondent's death in
1945.[11] Jarrell was a poet, and even then a prose stylist
of considerable accomplishment. Writing for a sophisticated magazine, he might have found it easy to ignore the passing of a mere journalist or to say
condescending things about him. But Pyle, as Jarrell
saw, was no mere journalist, and the qualities that
made him special happened to be the same qualities
that almost made Jarrell unique in his time. Pyle cared
about facts, Jarrell said; and he did not care about
style so much if he could just make the reader see and
feel as he did. Moreover, what Pyle looked at and responded to as he went from one combat theater to another was precisely what Jarrell looked at and
responded to all his life. "His affectionate amused understanding and acceptance of all sorts and levels of
people [derived] from his imaginative and undeviat-
ing interest in [and] observation of . . . people." These
were the words of Jarrell that best summarized his
view of Pyle's greatness and claim to truth. They constitute a garland that in his better moments (that is to
say, in most of them) Jarrell himself deserved to wear.

Notes

1. See *Randall Jarrell's Letters,* ed. Mary Jarrell (Boston: Houghton
Mifflin, 1985) 25–26.

2. *Kipling, Auden & Co.: Essays and Reviews 1935–1964* (New York: Farrar, Straus, 1980) 170–71.

3. *A Sad Heart at the Supermarket* (New York: Atheneum, 1962) 103; *Kipling, Auden & Co.* 312. This essay, "Poets, Critics, and Readers," reprinted in both volumes, was first published in *The American Scholar* (Summer 1959).

4. *Kipling, Auden & Co.* 312–13; *Sad Heart* 105.

5. "Some Lines from Whitman," *Poetry and the Age* (New York: Knopf, 1953) 112–32.

6. *Letters* 43.

7. *Poetry and the Age* 96–111.

8. *Kipling, Auden & Co.* 246.

9. At the outset Jarrell had announced that he would sometimes summarize or quote from things he had written previously.

10. *The Third Book of Criticism* (New York: Farrar, Straus, 1969) 314.

11. Reprinted in *Kipling, Auden & Co.* 112–21.

CHAPTER FOUR

Pictures from an Institution and the Children's Stories

R andall Jarrell's literary activity was not confined to poetry and criticism, though his achievements in these areas are the ones by which he is best remembered. He also published translations of fairy tales by the brothers Grimm and by Bechstein and, with great care and commitment to his task, produced translations of Chekhov's *The Three Sisters* and the first part of Goethe's *Faust*. Being virtually monolingual, Jarrell necessarily relied heavily, especially in the case of the Chekhov, on the translations of others to complete his two major projects, both of which were published after his death. During the last few years of his life he wrote, with equal care and commitment, four books for children—*The Gingerbread Rabbit*, *The Bat- Poet*, *The Animal Family*, and *Fly by Night*.

In addition, as he approached the peak of his powers, Jarrell produced, during 1952 and 1953, a

PICTURES FROM AN INSTITUTION AND
THE CHILDREN'S STORIES

truly major work of fiction, which was published in 1954. As its title suggests, *Pictures from an Institution* may be read as a series of portraits, and the first five of the seven chapter titles support that suggestion. Such portraits were characteristic of at least one other satiric novel about academic life that had appeared in the decade immediately following World War II (Mary McCarthy's *The Groves of Academe*), and it might seem that Jarrell was simply following an established lead. Moreover, since everything in his novel comes by way of the consciousness of a narrator, unnamed but with a wit that inevitably suggests Jarrell himself, some readers were tempted to think of *Pictures from an Institution* primarily as a brilliant "holiday" exercise by a talented poet who, having chosen to live and work on college campuses, suddenly found himself increasingly encumbered with material too rich to be ignored and decided to have fun with it. Jarrell's letters from the period indicate that he wrote his novel with the same combination of joy and serious care that provided the context for all the rest of his important work. John Crowe Ransom may have been closer to the truth than some realized when, two years after Jarrell's death, he wrote that *Pictures from an Institution* "just might be his great masterpiece."[1] In retrospect, one is inclined to agree. Certainly *Pictures from an Institution* towers above other novels about academic life and takes its place among modern

America's more distinguished achievements in comic fiction.

The plot is a simple one. Gertrude Johnson, distinguished southern novelist, comes to Benton, a fashionable college for women, with her adoring husband Sidney in tow, presumably to fill a semester's appointment as visiting teacher of writing. Privately, however, she has a second motive, which, except for Sidney, she shares only with the narrator: she hopes to collect material for a satiric novel about academic communities. Accordingly she cultivates the acquaintance of persons who seem likely to serve as good models and, with her professional objective to sustain her, manages to tolerate an existence which otherwise would have become unbearably tedious. Among her prospective subjects, in addition to the inevitable assortment of students, are President Dwight Robbins, boyish, faceless, and self-consciously unacademic, and his wife Pamela, from the Union of South Africa; the pretentious sociologist Jerrold Whittaker and his tasteless spouse Flo; Gottfried and Irene Rosenbaum, both musicians and Jewish expatriates from Austria; and Constance Morgan, the one near-innocent in the novel. Constance is a protégée of the narrator and his wife, but she is also attached to the Rosenbaums, who represent for her the epitome of Old World culture. As the story begins, Constance is serving as assistant secretary to President Robbins; as it ends, she decides to

PICTURES FROM AN INSTITUTION AND THE CHILDREN'S STORIES

resign and become secretary to Rosenbaum. That decision signals her maturation, which has progressed steadily during the course of the narrative and constitutes one cause for optimism about Benton. Even more gratifying, however, is the transformation that takes place in Gertrude, who at the end abandons her project to write a satiric novel, suggesting that instead she may write one about a writer.

Writing a novel about a writer is, in effect, what the narrator is doing throughout the novel. It is he, of course, who actually produces the set of pictures from an institution; but the work is also a unified novel about the narrator as a writer, somewhat less distinguished than Gertrude Johnson, who manages to transcend the arrogance that has led him, even as arrogance has led Gertrude, to regard fellow human beings as if they were static categories, dehumanized subjects for witty commentary. Near the end one sees that his playful identification of Gertrude with Satan of the Book of Job "walking up and down in Benton," has been transferred silently to himself.[2] By this time the reader sees that all along the narrator has been the principal person, going to and fro in the world of Benton and walking up and down in it. The book is the narrator's confession and his act of penance. The change that has come to Gertrude, partly as a consequence of his prodding, has helped to precipitate a similar change in him.

Moreover, in spite of the standard disclaimer proffered in the front of the book, the unnamed narrator is indeed a surrogate for Randall Jarrell. The world of Benton, like the world of the poems, is a part of Jarrell's world, compounded in large part of his own observations of men, women, children, and adolescent students. For that reason it is both interesting and valid, though not essential, to read *Pictures from an Institution* in relation to data from Jarrell's life, especially from the years he spent in Vanderbilt, Sarah Lawrence, and the Women's College of the University of North Carolina—the last two of which were, like Benton, exclusively for women when Jarrell knew them. Some of the experiences that went into the book have not been assimilated beyond recognition. For example, in the space of three pages there are references to a faculty member who cooked a hen over a collection of Bunsen burners, to another who "was paid by the National Association of Manufacturers to go around making speeches to Chambers of Commerce and never washed," and to still another who, in hopes of proving the inheritance of acquired characteristics, raised dachshunds that would sit up and beg before he or their mother taught them (96-98). All three of these are glimpses from Jarrell's own experiences in academia, and the last may be read as a nostalgic tribute to H. C. Sanborn, the Vanderbilt professor who experimented with goats before he went to dachshunds and whom a younger Jarrell found amusing but respected.

PICTURES FROM AN INSTITUTION AND THE CHILDREN'S STORIES

The presence of three such brief sketches so close together may be attributable to a passing mood of reminiscence. But the Rosenbaums appear throughout the novel, and these are, by Jarrell's acknowledgment, in part portraits of two dear friends, Heinrich Blücher and Hannah Arendt.[3] The less fully delineated—*caricatured* is the proper word—President Dwight Robbins of Benton owes a fair amount to President Harold Taylor of Sarah Lawrence.[4] More important, the narrator is again and again pointedly suggestive of Jarrell himself. Like Gertrude, Jarrell and his narrator had both lived in New York and acquired an easy familiarity with the city's ways and places. Like Jarrell, the narrator was in the air force during World War II, at Chanute Field, where his barracks mates called him "Tex" (177), and at an airfield near Tucson (89). Both Jarrell and the narrator subsequently became English teachers and poets and translators of Rilke (148). Both gave poetry readings (93-94). Both recognized the deadly artificiality of places like Benton and the complacency with which the inhabitants tended to think of them as "the real world," but both in time came to understand that such places sometimes also harbor persons of genius and humility who have discovered values which the world beyond the campus infrequently understands or tolerates.

Two such persons are the Rosenbaums, who live at Benton and accommodate to Benton's rhythms and patterns with good grace but remain apart from it.

Unassimilated, they feel no need to be anything other than themselves. Their patent genuineness in being simply what they are commends itself to the narrator and his wife and to young Constance Morgan, who thirsts for the kind of culture Benton professes to give but knows instinctively that she must seek it only from the Rosenbaums. The genuineness of the Rosenbaums commends itself also to Gertrude Johnson, who has come to Benton prepared to spare no one in her exposure of absurdities and pretensions. The Rosenbaums, however, are neither absurd nor pretentious. They preserve in their being the European culture that came into fine focus in the Vienna of Mahler and Freud, and so still breathe naturally the atmosphere that other people at Benton like to believe they have created in their secluded American retreat. Moreover, Gottfried and Irene Rosenbaum represent that rare amalgam of taste and learning that Jarrell spent a good part of his life reaching for and to a remarkable degree acquired: something that as a young man he had glimpsed in the lectures and conversation of his teacher Sanborn at Vanderbilt, and later in New York evenings with Hannah Arendt and Heinrich Blücher. It is fitting that Arendt should share the dedication of the novel with Jarrell's wife, for without her warmth and humor and wisdom there could never have been an Irene. Without an Irene to complement him, Gottfried Rosenbaum probably could not have performed credibly the

PICTURES FROM AN INSTITUTION **AND THE CHILDREN'S STORIES**

function that Jarrell gives him; and without the performance of that function at its center the novel would have been little more than a brilliant series of satiric pictures from an institution—the sort of thing Gertrude Johnson came to Benton to write, and indeed might have written had not two accidents stirred to life something in her long-suppressed humanity and shamed her into abandoning the whole project.

One of these accidents comes about as a consequence of Gertrude's casual and irresponsible observation that Constance Morgan must be having an affair with Gottfried. Constance, who cannot imagine herself as having an affair with someone she thinks of in the same terms as Mahler, Beethoven, or Goethe, is deeply shocked; and she courageously confronts Gertrude with a rebuke for the wrong she has done to Dr. Rosenbaum. Gertrude resents the man's invulnerability and has been planning even more hair-raising things to say about him. But she is so intimidated by the justice of the girl's challenge that she counters with an evasive "nobody would believe anything about *you*" and makes no further attempt to satirize Rosenbaum, who remains thereafter one of the pillars of Benton untouched by her wit. Another such pillar is Camille Turner Batterson, Gertrude's predecessor as teacher of creative writing at Benton, who is exposed to the satirist's knife when she returns briefly for a visit and then is presumably rendered invulnerable to satire by dying unexpectedly three months later. This is the second accident that frustrates Gertrude Johnson's design (actually the first chronologically), and Gertrude does not at first comprehend that it is such an accident or understand why the removal of Camille Batterson, whom she had scarcely known, should be so troubling to her. An explanation unfolds gradually as the novel works its way toward denouement.

At first Miss Batterson's death seems to make very little difference to Gertrude. She apparently has managed to capture for herself a portrait of the woman very much like the one the narrator gave the reader initially: that of a faintly ridiculous "maiden lady" from Virginia teaching at an eastern finishing school that is in many ways as southern as she is and certainly more Victorian than modern. Gertrude is a southerner herself and recognizes that she has in hand a good beginning for a superb piece of caricature, one that clearly seems destined to be "the ornament of the Book of Benton." Miss Batterson's sudden departure from the scene has frustrated any hope Gertrude may have entertained of further meetings; nevertheless she plunges ahead, bombarding the narrator with questions and demands for additional facts, secure in the conviction that all her satiric portrait will need for complete success is sufficient data. The fact that her subject in life was not a caricature but a warm and demonstrably mortal human being does not occur to her, for mortal-

PICTURES FROM AN INSTITUTION AND THE CHILDREN'S STORIES

ity itself is something that Gertrude has either declined to face or perhaps never even thought of. The narrator, seeing Gertrude's blindness in this regard, becomes increasingly aware that a disastrous shock for her is somehow imminent. Finally he assails her obliquely with the question, "Has anything happened to you since you've been at Benton?" At first Gertrude laughs at the suggestion that anything could possibly have happened to *her* in Benton. Then, dimly sensing the import of what he has asked her, she suddenly becomes evasive and finally admits, to herself as much as to the narrator, "Well, Miss Batterson died" (215). With that admission Gertrude Johnson's defenses collapse and both the portrait and the hard satiric novel that she has meant to write are doomed. The narrator, by contrast, though he seems not to have intended anything of the sort, suddenly finds himself on his way to writing a novel of his own. Miss Batterson's death, it appears, has "happened" to him also.

Miss Batterson herself does not appear in Jarrell's novel except retrospectively; but the narrator reports Gertrude's one meeting with her and frames it in a context that gives the woman a life more credible than any of those lives being presented directly. Like the Rosenbaums, Miss Batterson is the finished product of a regional maturation process that has resulted in a distinctive culture, the difference being that the root and flower of Miss Batterson's culture is Virginia rather than Austria. President Robbins, who never sees beyond the mask that southern gentility decrees a woman wear, was incapable of comprehending that some of the lady's seeming absurdities derived from principles that transcended his elementary "common sense" and logic. He regarded her as little more than an embarrassing legacy, and so when an unexpected turn of circumstances brought her an offer from a large midwestern university, he made no move "to stand in her way." Miss Batterson survived transplanting less than a year, and Benton, having already said good-bye to its friend, mourned perfunctorily.

Not Gottfried Rosenbaum, however, who the next day was on a plane to Charlottesville to attend the funeral. The scene that follows, related by him through the narrator, who ponders the meaning of it, is the heart and center of the novel. At the little Virginia town of Stanhope, where Battersons are buried even if they die elsewhere, Gottfried at first thinks he is simply paying the tribute of one fully individuated human being to another. Then Stanhope itself begins to intrigue him. What he finds there is unlike anything else he has experienced before—an agrarian society, literate but unlettered, graced with courtly manners, soft dialects, old and delicate furniture, beaten biscuits and country ham. He appreciates its integrity, feels almost at home in it, but also senses sadly that it is a world in passage, soon to disappear forever, even as his own Viennese world has disappeared.

PICTURES FROM AN INSTITUTION AND THE CHILDREN'S STORIES

The narrator adds a private reminiscence that he recalled a few days after Miss Batterson died. She had told him a story about her father, who was a small boy at the time of the Civil War and daily used to drive the family cows to pasture in a grassy meadow in the nearby swamp. The boy's charge was to keep watch all day at the entrance to the swamp and drive the cows home again in the late afternoon when they had finished grazing, and he frequently took up his post in the leafy branches of a large oak tree. In summer he always wore a straw hat; in cooler weather, an old shawl of his mother's. Unfortunately the day came when a scouting party of Union soldiers made camp beneath the tree, met the cows returning from the swamp, and killed and ate two of the creatures, one of them the boy's pet heifer, Elfie. Thus he had to spend a miserable night in the tree, enduring both the fear of being caught and the sadness of seeing his friend Elfie casually done away with by a group of unfeeling barbarians. That was the end of the story. The boy got away, of course, and lived to tell about it to his children; but the narrator realizes, now that Miss Batterson is gone, that it was always her face he saw beneath the boy's straw hat or framed in his mother's shawl. He does not need to say that he, like Gottfried Rosenbaum, saw what Benton had lost when Miss Batterson left for the midwest, where there was not even a Benton to protect in its perfunctory way the remnant of the life she loved, which the rest of the world could see only as something to be exploited—if the rest of the world could see it at all. It is to Gertrude Johnson's credit that in the end she draws back from exploiting this life that she has an all-but-suppressed capability for understanding; and it is to the unnamed narrator's credit that he comes to see, with Rosenbaum, the beauty and integrity of life which a person like Camille Batterson can bring to the world, even though Camille's life was one he would never seek to emulate. It is doubly to his credit that by the light of her memory he should begin to look for glimmers of light in the academic fog of blindness and self-satisfaction at Benton, and that he should succeed in building his own novel on something more than a detached satirist's scaffolding.

One must say something *more* than a detached satirist's scaffolding because the satirist is everywhere at work in *Pictures from an Institution*, and nowhere more brilliantly than in the next-to-last chapter, entitled "Art Night." Whatever model may have lurked in Jarrell's mind as he created Art Night at Benton, it resembles in a number of ways the Coraddi Arts Festival held each year during his tenure at the Women's College in Greensboro. *Coraddi* was the fine arts magazine there, published four times a year under the direction of student editors; and its arts festival, like the one at Benton, put on display such creative talent as had emerged on campus during the preceding

PICTURES FROM AN INSTITUTION AND
THE CHILDREN'S STORIES

twelve months. Like the festival at Benton it presented the talent of visiting notables in addition to that of students and, theoretically at least, was an occasion of considerable cultural stimulation for both campus and the surrounding community. Benton's Art Night consists of exhibitions of sculpture and painting, a special adaptation of Strindberg's *The Spook Sonata*, a dance-drama called *The Life of Nature* with a score by Gottfried Rosenbaum, and an address by a "distinguished visitor," Charles Francis Daudier, who gives his standard lecture on art and the democratic way of life. Jarrell's strategy for presenting all this is to manipulate the plot so that Gottfried, Gertrude (well fortified with Jack Daniel's), and the narrator go to the event together, with Gottfried observing, Gertrude making witty observations to whoever happens to be sitting or standing next to her, and the narrator commenting privately. The result is that Art Night is laid out for inspection and nothing is spared.

Jarrell's strategy here involves the risk of misdirecting the attention of more casual readers, whose delight in his deft ridicule of a pretentious spring ritual common in American small colleges may cause them to overlook subtler but more important developments taking place in the psyche of the narrator. To begin with, he is embarrassed both by what Gertrude says publicly (though privately he agrees with her on most counts) and by the malice with which she laces her wit. Her baiting of Miss Rasmussen, the absurd resident sculptor (who looks like a potato bug), pains him; her use of literary references to intimidate the local painter annoys him; and her unofficial performance during the lecture irritates both him and Gottfried. To their credit, however, it also makes them wonder whether in the past they too may not have been guilty of saying and doing similar things. Thus the satire on Art Night, which involves both Gertrude and the narrator, marks the divergence of their paths—hers in a departure from the center of the action which she has hitherto helped to define and his to a convergence with that action and a complete domination of it.

The last chapter, entitled "They All Go," reports the dispersal of the Benton community at the end of school: President Robbins to a fact-finding tour of Europe for the Rockefeller Foundation, Gertrude and Sidney to South America (with a renewed Guggenheim), the Whittakers to the Grand Canyon, and the Rosenbaums and Constance Morgan, now formally employed as Gottfried's secretary, to Cape Cod. The narrator has received a better offer and is leaving Benton permanently. After seeing the Rosenbaums off, he returns to campus to clean out his office. During the afternoon, his last on the now all-but-deserted campus, he meets Miss Rasmussen, the sculptor whose work on Art Night, mainly to counteract Gertrude

PICTURES FROM AN INSTITUTION AND THE CHILDREN'S STORIES

Johnson's unfeeling witticisms he had pretended to like. She insists that he come up to her second-floor studio to see her newest work, a recumbent human figure modeled out of a railroad tie and pivoted to revolve on a brass rod, like the needle of a compass. To his astonishment the narrator finds the piece meaningful and engaging and concludes that the woman, though still a potato bug, is a potato bug who has been visited by an angel. If he has misjudged her, he wonders, can he not have misjudged also the rest of Benton? The novel does not presume to answer this question directly—certainly not definitively. Clearly the narrator has misjudged Benton to some degree; but just as clearly, come September, Benton will begin another academic year with the same students and faculty—or reasonable facsimiles thereof—the same rituals, and the same daily round of petty absurdities. Yet the absurdities of Benton, he confesses near the end, have come to seem "almost, the ordinary absurdities of existence. Like Gertrude, I cherished my grievances against God, but to some of them I had become very accustomed" (269).

The narrator's abandonment of his impulses to satire reinforces an impression of reality in the work that is usually found only in the fiction of writers of great natural talent, maturity, and long experience. The artistry of Jarrell's performance here is explicable only by recognizing him as a writer who without conscious effort fulfilled Henry James's primary criterion, that of being one on whom nothing is lost. One suspects that any subsequent novel Jarrell might have written could have been only a sequel to this one. The voice and mind of the narrator—as in the poetry and the essays—are unmistakably those of Randall Jarrell: the vocabulary, the turn of phrase, the quips, the predilections and the prejudices, the learning, the insight into the complexities of the human psyche, the contempt for human stupidity that genius sometimes indulges in, and the reservoir of charity that, often in Jarrell's case, redeems contempt and makes it forgivable.

The Children's Stories

Toward the end of his life Randall Jarrell began writing children's stories. At the time that new direction for his work surprised some of his friends and dismayed others, but hindsight suggests that Jarrell was probably following the same daemon, or set of daemons, that had guided his course from the outset. Old themes continued to appear: the special perceptions of childhood, the epiphanic character of dreams, the loneliness of the creative spirit, the complementarity of the sexes, and the dignity of all creatures in the animal world. Some of the subjects were different, but not all of them; and the work as a whole in these sto-

PICTURES FROM AN INSTITUTION AND THE CHILDREN'S STORIES

ries exhibits compassion and modesty combined with the conviction that had guided all his other work: namely, that any representation of the universe, whether reported or presented in a fiction, must bear the impression and shape of a personal vision. Jarrell once observed playfully that no one could write better Kipling stories than Kipling. In the same sense no one could possibly write better stories of Jarrell's distinctive kind than Jarrell himself, and Jarrell wrote virtually nothing that did not bear a distinctive personal stamp from the beginning of his career to the end.

The label "children's stories" is misleading. Some critics inclined to be hostile said that children would never like these books. That is probably not true. Jarrell certainly expected *The Gingerbread Rabbit* to appeal to children and delighted in giving readings of it whenever groups of them could be assembled. *The Bat-Poet*, which came out in the same year, was not so successful when read aloud; but a great many adults bought it, presumably for children, in both hardback and paperback. *The Animal Family* and *Fly by Night*, both published posthumously, have not fared so well. But all four of Jarrell's last books are stories that capture and present an innocent, unprejudiced view of the process of the world like the one that comes immediately to the senses, without preconceived values, preordering, or limited directions and goals. They are adult versions of the stories that children themselves often make up when adults are not close by to correct them.

Of the four, *The Gingerbread Rabbit* most closely resembles a conventional children's book. One reason is the illustrations by Garth Williams, who had already served as illustrator for children's stories by E. B. White; another is the use of the gingerbread character, long associated with children's stories, particularly in America. The story begins with a series of events reminiscent of the old New England story of the gingerbread man, a story that most children know. The children who hear or read Jarrell's story are probably expected to have the other one in mind for ready comparison—at least to remember that the original figure hopped out of the oven and rushed out into the world to escape capture by a cow, a horse, and a group of threshers, only to fall victim to the manipulations of a clever fox. Jarrell's rabbit is not much wiser, but he is luckier. The woman who creates him gets her idea from a very large rabbit who wanders into the yard and stares at her without apparent fear until suddenly he startles both her and himself with a loud sneeze and then runs away. Thereupon she decides to make a rabbit out of gingerbread, exactly like the real one, for her little daughter, who has just gone off to school. The rabbit in Jarrell's story comes to life when the sunlight dries and warms him prematurely. Being precocious, he promptly engages the cooking utensils in conversation and learns that his destiny is that of all gingerbread: to be eaten. Thus he too runs away, to be chased by the woman, whom he takes to be a giant, and by the fox, whom he escapes only because the real rabbit comes along just in time to warn him. From here on the developments in the story are pure Jarrell. The woman eventually catches up with the fox, who loses all interest in his quarry when the woman explains that he is made of flour. Then, on the advice of a friendly squirrel, she returns home to make a rabbit *doll* for the little girl. The gingerbread rabbit goes home with the real rabbit and meets his wife, who is so charmed with her visitor that in no time at all she accepts him as a member of the family. The three of them live happily ever after in their home in the forest.

The most interesting thing about this story is Jarrell's repudiation of the moral embedded in the uncluttered succession of parallels in the original. The gingerbread man belonged to a world in which his destiny was clearly to be eaten by *somebody*; and because he tried to be something he wasn't, he had the misfortune to be eaten by a fox when he might just as easily have been eaten by a respectable housewife and her family or by a more congenial domesticated animal. The gingerbread rabbit is under no compulsion of any kind. It is the sunlight itself, not the woman or her oven, who has put life into his veins. He runs away not out of pride but in order to become what he legitimately may be, and his near disaster at the hands of the fox is the consequence of pardonable naïveté rather than cockiness (he thinks the fox is a special kind of rabbit). Moreover, in Jarrell's world one doesn't create figures of art in order to consume them. The woman apparently has not thought of *eating* the rabbit, and the fox abandons all notion of eating him when he learns that he isn't a real rabbit. The logic of the piece is one that almost every child who has ever loved a stuffed rabbit or teddy bear can readily understand: the icon loved achieves an independent life. One may repudiate the myth of Galatea as fancy and note that the statue that somes to life in *The Winter's Tale* is really the aging wife herself, but one cannot reject entirely the faith in the miraculous that this complex story invokes and does *not* repudiate. At least, it would not occur to a child to repudiate it.

The Bat-Poet is a different kind of story altogether. Here the child has no analogue in his head for comparison, and by the time he comes to the story he may very well have been prejudiced against bats by elders who see them in a category with snakes, spiders, and scorpions. It begins with a narrator telling about finding a cluster of bats on his front porch, much as Jarrell himself told of a similar experience dozens of times to any friend or colleague who would listen; but the narrator soon disappears, leaving only the story of the bat, who for reasons he does not fully understand declines to do as young bats are expected to do. That is,

PICTURES FROM AN INSTITUTION AND THE CHILDREN'S STORIES

he will not abandon the sanctuary of his infancy (a front porch) and retire to the barn with his brothers and sisters to begin communal bat life. Jarrell then sketches a credible and (for those who keep the analogy of the poet in mind) highly meaningful account of the young bat's discovery of day with all its activities and colors, things most bats are congenitally insensitive to. After a time the little bat begins to understand why during the night he has always been fascinated by the night-singing mockingbird, who fills his song with imitations of all the things he has seen and heard during the daytime, and he rushes to tell his brothers and sisters in the barn of the new delights he has discovered by way of the bird's song, or poem; but the bats in the barn are unimpressed.

By this time he has begun to devise poems of his own and accordingly feels a need for someone to recite them to. It occurs to him that he might recite them to the mockingbird; but when after tactful maneuvering he manages to get the bird's ear, he finds that the mockingbird-poet listens as a professional and can only compliment the young rival on his scansion. Gradually the bat-poet begins to recognize that true poets do not write for fame or for the approval of other poets, even if they be mockingbirds. Poetry for them is a way of telling the truth about the world; and sometimes for that, he suspects, they find no audience at all. Then he thinks of the poems he has written about the owl and the chipmunk, both true representations of parts of his own daytime world and both satisfying; but he thinks especially of his poem about the mockingbird, how he wars with jays, thrashers, and cats during the day and at night in his singing imitates his exploits so skillfully that hearers have difficulty telling which is bird and which is the world. Here he raises the question that for Jarrell had to be asked about any art that lays claim to significance and truth. For Jarrell the answer was, as he once said of Cézanne's painting of the mountain, that the realization of one necessarily involves the realization of the other. The bat-poet slowly comes to see that this must be his answer, too, and undertakes to write a poem about bats.

The result is the high point of the book, an attractive piece of thirty-four lines, which Jarrell included in *The Lost World* as "Bats." For this composition the bat-poet does achieve a proper audience, for the chipmunk on hearing it is speechless. He forgot he was listening to a poem, he says, and simply thought how queer (meaning also wonderful) it must be to be a bat. But the bat is still not entirely satisfied. Rejoicing that at last he has something that his fellow bats can understand, he flies off to the barn only to discover that they have all gone into their sleep of hibernation. He begins to recite the poem anyhow but falls asleep himself in spite of his intention, being at last both bat and poet, the poem and the world.

Jarrell's third children's book, *The Animal Family*, came out shortly after his death in October 1965. It

PICTURES FROM AN INSTITUTION AND THE CHILDREN'S STORIES

is the longest of the works for children and in some respects the most ambitious. The influence of Hans Christian Andersen is patent both in the nucleus of the story, that of the mermaid who married a human being, and in the development that Jarrell gave it. He had used the story once before, in the poem "A Soul," which first appeared in *The Seven-League Crutches*, but there he represented the relationship between sea maiden and man as an uneasy one at best. Here the man is a hunter, who has spent his life with animals, and the relationship between the two flourishes, once the mermaid overcomes her initial shyness.

One might read Jarrell's story as a metamorphosis of the Edenic myth; for the man, like Adam, lives happily in a paradise of wilderness and animals, over which he has complete dominion, and only belatedly comes to recognize that something necessary to his happiness is lacking. When he finds the mermaid, or rather when she finds him, he proceeds to exchange words with her—his land words for her sea words— but, like a child, she learns so rapidly that soon she is adopting *his* language and he is abandoning his efforts to learn hers. Then she consents to move a hundred and fifty steps from the ocean and live with him in a house, where she learns about furniture, fire, and clothing (which she considers an amusing affectation). Eventually the hunter begins to think of his parents and shows the maid a lace handkerchief that had belonged to his mother. She, however, has never seen another human being, so he carves figures of his parents for her out of wood. Immediately she sees the mother, who is wearing a long skirt that hides her legs, as someone exactly like herself and the image of the father as simply an image of the hunter. At this point the two are ready for parenthood.

Their first attempt to create a family, by adopting a bear cub, is not entirely satisfactory; so they adopt a lynx as well, but this too fails to fill their need. At last one day the bear and the lynx find a real boy sleeping beside a woman who lies dead in a boat that has drifted ashore. In time the boy becomes as much a part of the household as the two nonhuman animals, and the mermaid proceeds to instruct him in human ways, much as the hunter once instructed her. The story comes to a conclusion when the boy, having heard that he was found in a boat, takes that as a true account of his origin; but the hunter and the mermaid disabuse him. That is just a story for a child, they assure him; they have had him with them always.

Edenic myth or not, this story ends in a paradise of Jarrell's devising, or dreaming. One might call it uniquely his were it not for the matching dream that it has received in the drawings by Maurice Sendak. Jarrell's handling of the story produces resonances that find a complementary response in many readers, old as well as young. *The Gingerbread Rabbit* may remain for some at the level of folk tale; *The Bat-Poet* may pass as a fable about the situation of the poet. *The*

PICTURES FROM AN INSTITUTION AND THE CHILDREN'S STORIES

Animal Family, however, approaches the level of universal symbol, as Jarrell's better poems do; and given its skill of execution, it deserves to stand with these.

Fly by Night was the last of Jarrell's children's books. He completed it in 1963, but the book did not appear until 1976, when it was published with illustrations by Maurice Sendak, who had done the remarkably complementary illustrations for *The Bat-Poet* and *The Animal Farm*. The illustrations for *Fly by Night*, however, all but overshadow the text, which is thin in comparison with the two previous books, though it has the same relevance to significant aspects of Jarrell's life. Like them, it reflects his affinity with all forms of nonhuman animal life; and in addition it makes explicit his lifelong fascination with flying creatures and with flying in general. Moreover, it reveals, as poignantly as anything Jarrell had written before, a sometimes suppressed but never entirely resolved yearning for the comfort of a stable mother figure in his life.

Like *The Bat-Poet* this story begins by citing a tangible connection with the Jarrell home in Guilford College, North Carolina, here in the form of a brief set of directions for the traveler coming there from nearby Greensboro. This is where the boy David lives, with his parents, a dog named Reddy (the name of the pet rabbit in Jarrell's childhood), and a cat named Flour. In the daytime David is like any other boy. At night he can fly, or thinks he can, for on some nights he seems to rise up from his sleep and soar or float past his sleeping parents, whose dreams he can see, past Reddy, whose dreams he can almost see, and out into the night world. There the animals speak to him in rhyme; the cat and three dancing mice use tercets; a rabbit eating vegetables in his father's garden uses a quatrain. Farther on he encounters six woolly sheep and three ponies; and finally he meets another flying creature, a female owl, who hospitably invites the flying David to go along with her to the nest and be "an owl till morning." There in the top of a hollow oak he meets three owlets, watches them eat the fish their mother has brought, and listens while the owl tells her charges a bedtime story of some eighty-eight lines, for the most part in terza rima, about a lonely owlet who found a sister to play with.

This story within the story is, in effect, a dream within a dream and a story about the flying David who has become "an owl till morning;" but it introduces elements (the dead owl and the newly found sister) that have no parallel in the main story and remain unexplained at the end to tease and trouble our minds. When she has finished her story, the female owl guides David back to his own bedroom, where he drifts into a sleep that lasts until the sun wakes him. Then he runs to the kitchen to find his mother making pancakes. Embracing her, he tries unsuccessfully to tell her about the adventures of the night; but as he looks into her

PICTURES FROM AN INSTITUTION AND
THE CHILDREN'S STORIES

face, he thinks for a moment that she looks like the mother owl of his dream, if it was a dream.

The echoes of earlier poems are obvious here. One thinks of the flying sequences in "The Night Before the Night Before Christmas," of the bird imagery and the longing for a sister in "The Black Swan," and of the ambiguous dream transformations of the mother in "A Quilt-Pattern." Numerous explications might be made of this poem in prose, but *Fly by Night"* is primarily a self-sufficient symbol, one that brings into orderly relation needs, desires, and fears that were Jarrell's, certainly, but never his alone. The universality of the work, with or without the Sendak illustrations, becomes apparent as one reads and finds that his own needs, desires, and fears have been set concretely before him.

Notes

1. John Crowe Ransom, "The Rugged Way of Genius," *Randall Jarrell, 1914-1965,* ed. Robert Lowell, Peter Taylor, and Robert Penn Warren (New York: Farrar, Straus 1967) 165.

2. Randall Jarrell, *Pictures from an Institution* (New York: Knopf, 1954) 131-34, 270. Page references within the text are to this edition.

3. *Randall Jarrell's Letters,* ed. Mary Jarrell (Boston: Houghton Mifflin, 1985) 392.

4. *Letters,* 288, 366-67.

CHAPTER FIVE

The Later Poems

*T*he *Seven-League Crutches*, published in 1951, when Jarrell was thirty-seven years old, marked the end of a first stage in his maturation as a poet. His war volumes, *Little Friend, Little Friend* and *Losses*, had contained poems, notably "Lady Bates," "The Märchen," and "The Snow-Leopard," that continued the remarkable exploitation of technique and exploration of theme begun in *Blood for a Stranger*; but in many ways Jarrell's war poetry was a digression that did not significantly advance the basis for his claim to a permanent reputation. *The Seven-League Crutches*, with such poems as "Girl in a Library," "Seele im Raum," "A Quilt-Pattern," and "The Sleeping Beauty," made it clear to most observers that a poet of major stature was in the wings; and *The Woman at the Washington Zoo*, published nine years later, brought that poet to the center of the public stage and made the National Book Award that he received in that year not merely appropriate but almost inevitable. This new

THE LATER POEMS

collection of poems represented the full flowering of the rich poetic talent that Vanderbilt's Fugitives had recognized and encouraged more than two decades before—a talent which, since that time, had increasingly been seen to have a distinctive character of its own and the power to develop independently.

Some commentators have puzzled over the nine-year hiatus between *The Seven-League Crutches* and *The Woman at the Washington Zoo.* Suzanne Ferguson has a judicious discussion of this matter which interested readers should consult.[1] Suffice it to say here that Jarrell was not idle during the period between 1951 and 1960. In addition to the mature collection of poems and translations in *The Woman at the Washington Zoo* he wrote his only novel during these years and brought out his first collection of essays, *Poetry and the Age,* which some consider a landmark in American literary criticism. He also taught at Greensboro and elsewhere, lectured widely, and served as poetry consultant at the Library of Congress. More important, however, Jarrell seems to have been developing quietly a new direction for his poetic talent that would not bear its fruit until the year of his death, when he published *The Lost World.* It is regrettable but in retrospect not surprising that critics gave that last book a mixed reception.

The Woman at the Washington Zoo is a book that Jarrell had prepared his readers and critics to understand. The first three poems in it bring together themes (notably that of the woman denied full humanity), techniques, and strategies that he had employed successfully in previous poems, but never before with such intensity. In the title poem, as in "Seele im Raum" from *Seven-League Crutches*, he uses the persona of a woman to deliver a monologue that reveals an unhappy spirit desperate for the freedom to participate in life.[2] He gives her the familiar pentameter line, at least in the beginning, but even at the beginning the lines themselves exhibit a restlessness, an impulse to become something else, that points to and confirms her cry at the end, "Change me, change me!" The woman at the zoo is that most familiar sight on the streets of the city of a thousand bureaucracies: the female office worker, circumspect, faceless, undistinguished; and Jarrell places her in situations that accentuate her drabness: on Embassy Row, where gorgeously dressed Asian women brighten the streets, and in the zoo in Rock Creek Park, where the animals in their natural coats, even caged as they are, seem to have clearer identities than the people who watch them. The woman is at least aware of her predicament, and she meditates on the absurdity of a life in which being unnoticed is a virtue and on the irony of a situation where, trapped like the animals but in a cage of monumental buildings and fountains, she can find no one interested in who or what she is. The animals in their cages at least attract scavengers, she thinks, who come to eat the remnants of their feedings—sparrows, pigeons, rats, and sometimes vultures; and she pathetically entertains the fantasy that the red-capped turkey buzzard in the foxes' cage might be a fairy-tale prince in disguise, come to step to her as man, recognize the princess beneath the navy "null," and miraculously effect a transformation.

The theme of repressed womanhood is also at the center of the second poem in the volume, "Cinderella," which, according to Ferguson, Jarrell in a reading at the National Poetry Festival in 1962 described as being about "the underside" of his heroine.[3] Jarrell's Cinderella has long since passed beyond fairy godmother, prince, and glass slipper. Now dead and damned she sits by the fires of Hell, keeping company with that dark old woman, the Devil's mother; and she recalls bitterly the life she has led as an exalted female object in a man's world. Better this, she thinks, than to grow old and sit by the prince's fire telling stories to his children and his children's children.

The woman in the third poem, "The End of the Rainbow," is like Cinderella in that she too has repudiated the role of wife and mother; but this woman is not dead, and the hell she inherits is a pleasant establishment, part house and part gift shop, on the coast of Southern California, where she lives with her black dwarf Pekingese, Su-Su.[4] The woman, ironically named

Content, comes originally from Massachusetts, where some of her inheritance is held "in trust to the end of time." She reflects that life is not held in trust and wonders whether it can ever be lived so. The suitor whom she rejected years ago, for financial reasons, now haunts her imagination and her memory as the Frog-Prince of fairy tale. He "goggles at her from the bottom of the mail-slot," comes to her in fantasy in the guise of a seal-lover or merman, and appears in dreams as a male visitor freshly shaved and smelling of peppermint, standing in water with water babies swimming at his feet. No matter; her Frog-Prince is now married to a frog and has a family of little frogs, to whom he sometimes tells the story about how he once nearly married a mortal. Mortal herself, and now aging, the woman has Su-Su, Ralph Waldo Emerson and Mary Baker Eddy, an occasional female friend, and her painting; nevertheless she sees herself as wandering through the suburbs with a begging-bowl, calling, *Untouched! Untouched!* She asks Death, who seems increasingly to be a companion, whether her life has not been, in a way, a success; Death hesitantly replies with the equivalent of perhaps. She begins to think that possibly she has dug for gold at the wrong end of the rainbow; but Su-Su, sleeping in the doorway of the gift shop, has no such misgivings. His dreams and his reality are one.

No summary, of course, can give an adequate notion of a poem like "The End of the Rainbow," which is a mixture of observer's commentary, reported dream, reflection, and transactions presented in their immediacy. The effect is something like perceiving an event presented in both temporal and spatial extension and simultaneously from more than one point of view. The objective of the poem, realized here with a fair degree of success, is to present an illusion of reality exemplifying a theme that Jarrell explored in numerous contexts and at varying levels throughout his work: namely, the increasing inability of the individual human being participating in the flux of existence to perceive with certainty the significance of his or her passage at any given point. Retrospect does bring some things into focus, and experience of that can encourage the hope that retrospect will also redeem some of the pain of the present; but beyond that we can at most hope for full involvement in the process. This is what the girl in the library dreams of. It may well be one reason Jarrell himself was never unwilling to go to a war he deplored. It is what the woman at the zoo cries for, and it is what Cinderella and Content in her gift shop think they have missed. It is also what Jarrell addresses himself to in the four short pieces that he selected to follow "The End of the Rainbow" in his fifth volume of poems.

The first two of these are among the eight poems in *The Woman at the Washington Zoo* that Jarrell had published previously.[5] "In Those Days," a piece in four rhymed quatrains that first appeared in 1953, has the substance and tone of a personal utterance. The speaker looks back to a youthful courtship, conducted in defiance of not only the usual restrictions but also an unusually severe winter, remembers how poor and miserable they were at the time, and reflects how much better it all seems at a distance. "The Elementary Scene" goes back to 1935, when Jarrell was twenty-one, and it puts together a series of images from his relatively recent and apparently unhappy past: a pale autumn sun, dried grass, a solitary cow in the field, a rotting pumpkin. He recalls, too, how such images troubled him as a child, but again mature awareness, the future to that distant past, mends everything and this time makes poetry of it.

"Windows," a new poem much more serious than either of these, picks up a variation on the same theme, this time one that Jarrell had adumbrated in "The Orient Express" from *The Seven-League Crutches.* In that earlier poem the speaker had looked out of the window of the train, caught the passing scenes, and longed to know the unknown (and un-wanted) life behind them. Here the speaker wanders through snow-covered streets on a moonlit night and watches the life that goes on (to him silently) in the in-dividual houses. There is a pattern or ritual to their lives, he believes, of which these people are unaware, and he longs to be a part of that pattern—to see what the woman is sewing, to hear what the man is reading

THE LATER POEMS

in his evening paper. He thinks these people are like dead actors that uncomprehending children watch in an old movie on television on a rainy afternoon. Just as the children watch a strange world that existed before they themselves existed, so the speaker watches these "windowed ones within their windowy world" move about without apparent reason, imagines that they are immune to the troubles that beset him, and like a child watching television dreams of entering their untroubled existence. It is interesting that the redeeming distance in this case is not a temporal distance, but it is likened to a temporal distance in the image of the children watching an old movie on television. In both cases retrospect, or looking back from a distance, permits one to believe in the existence of a purposeful pattern that is not apparent to someone involved in the tensions and pressures of the immediate passage.

"Aging," another new poem, looks forward toward the seemingly more accessible poetry of Jarrell's last years. The speaker here is a man of Jarrell's age (mid-forties), and he remarks on the increasingly rapid passage of time as one grows older. This is a commonplace observation, though great poetry has been made of it from time to time, and Jarrell at least makes interesting poetry of it. Time was, he notes, when he had leisure for making things; and with all his early free time he did, in fact, make himself. Then after a pause he acknowledges that even so he still has not had time enough to remake his "childish heart," the heart that yearns for an "always" to make whatever it seeks to make and yearns also for impossible perfection: that is, not merely for time but for eternity. One conclusion that this brief poem invites is that even though the human condition remains a limited one, the human rage for permanence and order is both unquenchable and insatiable. In short, the speaker dreams of transcendence and an escape from mortality.

"Aging" is not one of Jarrell's better poems, and it serves mainly as a transitional piece within the context of this particular collection. It is followed by one of the more remarkable pieces in the Jarrell canon, "Nestus Gurley," a poem about his paper carrier, the son of the superintendent of the physical plant at the University of North Carolina at Greensboro. He uses the boy's real name and adds to that verifiable datum a collection of equally verifiable particulars: Nestus's habit of whistling or humming half out of tune, his derby hat, and the troop of dogs and children that joins him along the way and joyously helps him complete his route. Then he inserts a section in which the reader hears one of Jarrell's daughters in a brief conversation with Nestus as he collects for a month with five Sundays in it. After that come four sections in which the narrator is led progressively to a contemplation of eternity and, in playful contrast with the

THE LATER POEMS

poem immediately preceding, some limitations of eternity itself.

The implicit context for these sections is the practice of the Moravian Church, still flourishing in Jarrell's North Carolina and represented magnificently by the reconstructed town of Old Salem in nearby Winston-Salem. The relevant data in the poem are the love-feast with coffee and sweet buns, held in anticipation of Christmas, and the multipointed paper Moravian star that Piedmont North Carolinians, non-Moravians and Moravians alike, delight in hanging over their doorways during the holiday season. The star symbolizes both the Christmas star of Bethlehem and the morning star of Revelation 22:16, which is frequently interpreted as symbolic of Christ at the Second Coming and thus a prelude to the Last Judgment. The Moravians take special note of the latter in their Easter celebration, which begins with a German band parading through the streets waking sleepers with hymns. All are expected to follow and congregate for a service at the graveyard at sunrise, symbolic of resurrection on the last day.

In the first of the last four sections Nestus Gurley is facetiously presented as bringing either the Morning Star or the Evening Star, depending on which paper he happens to be delivering (he is a carrier for both the Morning *News Record* and the Evening, and thus delivering the judgment on the world that any honest newspaper delivers in reporting the irreversible account of things done and things left undone. This is the real Nestus Gurley.

The Nestus Gurley of the speaker's dreams appears in the next section. Here he brings news of the impending judgment of Christian belief (the bombers bent on destruction have desisted at the appearance of the morning star of Revelation), and the speaker, waking, thinks of a recent visit to Old Salem, where he heard the children singing, received the sweetened bun, still not eaten, and bought the Moravian star for his door. He has enjoyed these symbols as any tourist might, has not committed his own belief to any of them. In the third section he sees Nestus Gurley marching across the lawn like the Angel of Judgment, passing the pet cat returning from nightly adventures and tossing his morning paper, folded in the way some carriers still fold their papers, suggestive of a Napoleonic three-cornered hat. The speaker steps to the lawn, picks up the "hat" and figuratively puts it on (actually he simply unfolds the paper), and reflects that in its function the paper is not altogether unlike a madman's Napoleonic hat. It is after all full of another "dawn" of happenings that mark us as the madmen we "of our days and institutions" are. It brings judgment, not the final apocalypse perhaps, but a revelation or "dawn" nevertheless.

All this is playful, of course; but the playfulness of the last section, or stanza, becomes serious in a way

THE LATER POEMS

that some readers may miss. The speaker goes on to reflect that hearing Nestus Gurley on the lawn of a spring morning may be likened to a belief that Moravians and some other Christians hold: that at the end of things, when we lie cold in our graves, we may hear the angel approaching with his trumpet to rouse the dead to face judgment. If such a thing comes to pass, he wonders, will he be able to say, "It is Nestus Gurley"?

Here the figure becomes inverted, and eternity becomes a metaphor for Nestus Gurley—something that the general development of the poem has hardly helped us to anticipate. Even so, the unexpected turn of things by which the paper carrier has suddenly become the ultimate reality, relegating the Christian's eternity to the role of insubstantial dream, is wholly characteristic of Jarrell and in the tongue-in-cheek play of the poem quite acceptable. Nevertheless, it still suggests that the images by which we in the western world have symbolized most things (our collection of fables, myths, and märchen) are inadequate in proportion as they do what many of our religions would have them do: focus attention upon a dream of reality rather than upon the reality that the senses present, the only reality anyone can really know. Thus, Jarrell says wittily (that is, facetiously and seriously at the same time), if there is indeed such a thing as resurrection, and some morning he is lying cold in his grave (the grave lit by nothing more than hope), and he hears the angel approaching, may he not indeed exclaim, "Why, it's only Nestus Gurley, after all!" and rise up to get his copy of the *Daily News.*

"Nestus Gurley," for all its playfulness, may well be the most Rilkean, subtly if not overtly, of Jarrell's poems up to this point, consisting as it does of a fundamentally serious attempt to realize the "inwardness" of things and events (i.e., the true Nestus Gurley and his action) and its repudiation of western humanity's inclination to subordinate things in their presentational immediacy to some purified essence from which we fancy they derive. In any case, "Nestus Gurley" serves better than some of Jarrell's more obviously Rilkean pieces to introduce one of the significant features of *The Woman at the Washington Zoo:* a collection of twelve translations, nine of them from Rilke.

The group includes a lovely piece by Radauskas that has affinities with the selections from Rilke, a translation of the archangels' song from Goethe's *Faust,* and a translation of Eduard Mörike's "Forest Murmurs," which signals Jarrell's continuing affection for the German fairy tale; but these are incidental to the design of the book. The selections from Rilke pick up themes that had already appeared in it or look forward to themes to be explored in the last eleven poems. For example, it may be that "The Great Night," one of Rilke's poems published posthumously, was in Jarrell's mind when he composed "Windows." Both present a speaker who longs for identification with the world before him but feels excluded. Jarrell in his own poem dreams of ultimately being received into the lives beyond the windows. Rilke in this poem and in one other that Jarrell translates here, "Evening," takes comfort in acceptance offered by the all-encompassing night, a development that Jarrell may have had in mind when he wrote his poem about the psychiatrist, "Jerome." Rilke's early "Lament" presents a longing for something not mortally affected by mutability, much like the longing Jarrell expressed in "Aging." Rilke's great poem "Childhood" probably lies behind many of Jarrell's poems, early and late; and his decision to include a translation of it in this volume must have had something to do with his resuscitation of the very early poem "The Elementary Scene" to include with the more sophisticated pieces of his maturity. A similar relationship likely exists between his translation of Rilke's "Requiem for the Death of a Boy" and "A Ghost, a Real Ghost," another early poem, the last four lines of which read like a commentary on the German poem.

The value of the translations is their intrinsic excellence, both as extraordinarily faithful presentations of poetry that before had not been fully accessible to readers of English and as poems highly appropriate for inclusion in *The Woman at the Washington Zoo.* Great translators have not always been great linguists.

Yeats ventured to translate Sophocles: Pound, Anglo-Saxon poetry; and Eliot, St. -J. Perse. Jarrell's competence in his favorite foreign tongue was admittedly slight, but his knowledge of German was not quite so limited as he himself maintains in "Deutsch Durch Freud." The poem itself is evidence to the contrary. Still, for all practical purposes, he was monolingual, unable to converse in any language but his own and at least mildly disconcerted when visiting any country where English was not spoken widely. He understood the nature of language, however, and he understood poetry; and consequently his experiments in translation, which include translations from French poetry, especially Corbière, translations of German folk tales, a translation of part 1 of Goethe's *Faust*, and a translation of Chekhov's *Three Sisters*, have stood up remarkably well and have received praise from critics and poets alike.[6]

The last eleven poems in *The Woman at the Washington Zoo* vary widely in quality and interest. Only three deserve to be included among Jarrell's better pieces; the others are either simply minor works or works that, for one reason or another, he did not include in *Selected Poems*. An example of the latter is "Deutsch Durch Freud," the amusing piece from 1950 in which the speaker, presumably Jarrell himself, laments his inadequate knowledge of German. German is his favorite country, he begins, meaning by that his favorite world is the one that he glimpses, though imperfectly, through the medium of the German language. Fancifully, he says he must be the log which German fairies leave in the crib when they steal away the true child, in his case presumably one who was destined to *be* German and speak and write the language. Thus, cut off from his patrimony, he is doomed to stumble about in a world where everything—mice, rats, tables, chairs, even the nightingale—everything, and every person but him, speaks German. Even so, simply hearing and feeling the words—for example, when he reads Rilke in love and trust, without a dictionary—he sometimes feels as if he were receiving a benediction from the hand of God, and with that blessing is prepared to enter directly into communion with the mysteriously wonderful universe that German, the supreme language among languages, has created. It is better to know and love German in this way, he concludes, than to know the language as plodding students know it.

In another early piece the speaker is not a changeling, German or otherwise, but, as the title suggests, "A Ghost, a Real Ghost." This poem may have resulted from Jarrell's preoccupation with Rilke's "Requiem for the Death of a Boy," which, as has been noted, provided the text for one of the most successful translations in *The Woman at the Washington Zoo.* The child in Rilke's poem, now a ghost, remembers joyfully his identification with things that he has learned about during his experience in the world—apples, toys, coffee cups, the sky—and wistfully wonders whether in his new state he will have to learn about the same things all over again. By contrast, the ghost in Jarrell's poem remembers principally the pain of living and notes sadly that the pain persists even though he can no longer see himself in a mirror. He thinks of the nursery rhyme about the sad little woman who fell asleep by the stile and lost her identity when pranksters cut off her skirt; and he recalls wondering as a child where the woman went afterward. Now he knows that she went nowhere. Like himself, she simply no longer had access to a world she nevertheless could not forget.

The activation of the memory of a ghost is also the ostensible subject of still another early poem, the enigmatic "The Girl Dreams That She Is Giselle," in which the speaker, the young girl herself, imagines that, like the heroine of the ballet, she has been commanded to remember the life she has left. The pain of living remembered haunts "The Traveler," another early poem that so far has defied satisfactory explication by critics; and the same pain is clearly involved in "The Sphinx's Riddle to Oedipus," with its further affirmations that to see the truth of our lives carries an obligation to speak, yet to speak is to be alone. The pain is assuaged in a typically Jarrellian fashion in

THE LATER POEMS

"The Lonely Man," a poem that appeared for the first time in *The Woman at the Washington Zoo*. Here the speaker regularly walks up and down his block, where he has nothing more than a nodding acquaintance with the other people who live there; but he knows the animals: a gray cat, who sits impassively on his pavement, as indifferent to neighbors as to his owners; a friendly collie and a half-Persian, who seem to be concerned about their mutual friend, an old and seemingly blind white cat that sits in the window; and a spaniel who guards his territory. Some of these, certainly the collie and the Persian, mitigate the man's loneliness and take their place with all the other friendly animals Jarrell celebrated in his work. Even so, not all animals are so amiable; he suspects the gray cat, for example, of learning to be a man.

The most successful new poems in the last third of *The Woman at the Washington Zoo* are "Jamestown," "Jerome," and "The Bronze David of Donatello." The first of these calls to mind the satiric Jarrell of the war years. Here the speaker, an adult of presumably advanced years, looks back on the "kindergarten" image of true Americanism that has served him for most of his life, a view romantically epitomized by the familiar engravings of Captain John Smith's rescue from death by the native Indian maiden Pocahontas. The complex of sequels to that presumably historical event is hazy in his mind, but equally romantic. In any case, the precise details do not concern him; it is enough to believe that the savage Indian recognized instinctively the propriety of white America's assumption of control in the New World. In the third of the three irregular unrhymed stanzas in that poem, however, Jarrell has his transplanted European meet a witch in the woods and in fairy-tale fashion ask her to "make me what I am." The witch replies that his request is pointless; he has tended to make the whole world after the same kindergarten image by which he has lived. He should be asking instead for an answer to the question, "What am I?" Presumably the man does ask, and her response in a three-line envoi is simply that a rocket can now fly from Jamestown to Washington, D.C., in eleven minutes. In several of the poems in *Losses* Jarrell had made similar points about the effect of America's romantic self-image on the extension of World War II. Here he applies it to wars of the future, with even more chilling effectiveness—many times more chilling, it must seem to us, now that the flying time for rockets needs to be revised drastically, downward.

"Jerome," the next-to-last piece in the volume, might be described simplistically as a poem on the same theme as "The Lonely Man": animals are more reliable and more comforting than people. Here it is suggested they are also more reliable than angels or whatever source of inspiration or guidance we may choose to believe in. The poem sets two figures before

THE LATER POEMS

us. The first is a modern psychiatrist, now aging and increasingly lonely; the second is the great theologian and translator St. Jerome, trying in his desert cell to write at the dictation of the angelic voice. The two figures are separated for the most part, and the second comes to us as a dream of the first; but at various points in the poem the two coalesce briefly, and we see them as parallel images of a single impulse or action. As the poem begins, the psychiatrist is at the end of a wearying day (presumably near the end of a wearisome life also). After he has dismissed his last patient, he boils an egg for his evening meal and sits down to meditate, but his own problems and those of his patients give him no rest. Finally at midnight he lies down on the couch where his patients have lain and whispers his own problems to the listening night, which is the only confessor the secular psychiatrist can turn to. After a time he drifts into sleep and dreams of St. Jerome, his counterpart in another time and place.

Actually he dreams of the lion whom Jerome befriended and who ever after remained to guard his benefactor. The lion gives a description of Jerome very much like the ones we see in Renaissance paintings and engravings: the old man in his retreat, surrounded by all the accouterments of the scholar-saint and by his friends, the wild beasts of the desert, including, of course, the lion himself. In his left hand Jerome holds a stone, with which he beats his breast for continual penance, and in his right, a pen in readiness for whatever word the hovering angel may bring. Yet the angel does not speak to Jerome any more than the night speaks to the psychiatrist.

To understand this poem fully the reader should glance briefly at another translation of Rilke, one which Jarrell made for *The Seven-League Crutches* but did not include in *Selected Poems.* This is "The Olive Garden," in which Christ at Gethsemane, near the end of his life and "alone with all men's sorrow," reaches for the God whom he can no longer find. The poet-speaker recalls hearing it reported that an angel came later to console him; but he himself does not believe that any angel came, only the indifferent night that comes to all and sadly endures until morning. Thus in Rilke's poem there is no sign, no event, to suggest that the life of the man Jesus had a special significance. His life, like other lives, merely came to an end, with friends and relatives turning away because, as Robert Frost once put it in another connection, they were not the one dead—or dying.

So it is in "Jerome"; both the angel and the night are silent. It is not surprising that the secular psychiatrist in a post-Christian age receives no intimation of significance for his life; but western tradition has it that saints are more fortunate and frequently have angelic ministers to comfort and reassure them in their moments of uncertainty. Jerome's lion, of course, knows better; and here it is the lion, an animal and so denied benefits of the Christian dispensation, who reports on the saint who has been canonized by other mortal men. To the lion, who knows nothing of religion and its angels, Jerome is simply the man whom he loves. It is much the same with Jerome's counterpart, the psychiatrist, who is momentarily rejuvenated by the cheer of morning light and goes out for his walk. He stops briefly at the grocer's and then proceeds to the zoo, where he meets his friends the lynx and the leopard, and like a modern Jerome holds out a gift of raw liver to the lion, who licks his hand in return. Both psychiatrist and saint, the poem implies, in their exchange of affection with these unpretentious creatures of earth, have all the meaning in their lives one could ask for.

For the final poem in *The Woman at the Washington Zoo* Jarrell offered an unusual meditation on a familiar work of art, "The Bronze David of Donatello." Histories say that Donatello's masterpiece was the first life-sized, free-standing nude to appear since ancient times, but Jarrell sees only the timeless, androgynous, almost frivolously bonneted figure improbably represented as having defeated and killed the formidable Goliath. The style is that of Jarrell at his best—a series of irregular lines, with only a hint of the unrhymed iambic pentameter that had characterized earlier work, now free to assume shape and length appropriate to their function in the movement of the whole. The movement is that of a trained eye proceeding from one pair of incongruous details to another, the giant sword in the graceful hand, the tasseled headdress and the naked body, the girlish boy perched upon the head of his victim, "like a bird/ Standing on something it has pecked to death." Upon this head, the speaker imaginatively proposes, the boy dances in triumph like some figure upon a spire; yet the real victor in this poem is not David but the slain Goliath, suddenly and without the pain of anticipation relieved of the burden of living. It would be easy to see in the final line, with its "sleep blessed, blessed death," a rejection of the life that threatened to devastate the unfortunate woman at the Washington Zoo and dispirited the speaker in "The Lonely Man" and the aging psychiatrist in "Jerome"; but such a reading here would probably be wrong. David is simply victorious youth, in callowness not unlike the figure of Ganymede on the Nashville Parthenon for which the boy Jarrell served as a model,[7] unaware of the reverses, losses, and disappointments that inevitably will outnumber successes and sadden his last days. Goliath, by contrast, has been brought low at the peak of his illusion of invincibility, and his defeat, his sleep, his death are blessings that are reflected in the calm satisfaction on the reposeful face at the base of the statue. Goliath will never

THE LATER POEMS

grow old; and he can never know defeat, for this fatal encounter was accomplished before he had time to be aware of it. It is significant, as the speaker notes, that there is no impression of the stone on his forehead. In short, this poem, though it is richly expressive of youthful exuberance and confidence, speaks wisely of a mature man's awareness of the pain that is the inevitable sequel to youth's joys and of the mortality that young David has not yet tasted.

The Lost World came out in 1965, the year of Jarrell's death, and, as has been noted, produced a mixed response. The autobiographical nature of the title poems disturbed some reviewers, and none of the other "large" poems seemed comparable in quality to the best of *The Seven-League Crutches* and *The Woman at the Washington Zoo*. The volume contained poems on a variety of subjects, most of which, admittedly, Jarrell had treated before with more intensity. Nevertheless, it had a coherence that early reviewers missed, and it was the product of a real advance in Jarrell's awareness of what a serious poet does. The phrase "the lost world" does refer to Jarrell's vanished California boyhood, to be sure, and it also reflects the activity at a Hollywood studio where Jarrell caught glimpses of the monster figures used in the filming of Arthur Conan Doyle's *The Lost World*. The comprehensive meaning of the term includes any world or story that human beings may create out of the hetero-

geneous data that life proffers, and that meaning is set
forth in one poem in the collection that serves as a
philosophical center of sorts for the whole.

On the surface "The House in the Wood" seems to
look back to Jarrell's earlier examinations of the Hansel and Gretel story, but that connection is only incidental. The physical situation in this late poem is a
deep, presumably endless, wood with houses ranged
in front of it. Within the wood, is the House in the
Wood, which the speaker identifies as his own. In
summer, he says, the wood provides sounds that he
puts into his song. When he is awake he takes walks in
it, revisits the cage and the witch's oven which once
were meaningful to him; but as the light fades and the
foliage falls away, as it always does both at the end of
the day and at the end of the year, he begins to see the
wood and the house within it for what they are. The
wood is secondary being, the sensible world unshaped
by fiction or art, pathless, without houses, and without coherence; yet wherever he walks there, he always
comes eventually to the House in the Wood, the house
where the self lies wooden, motionless, perhaps extended forever in space and time, "at the bottom of the
world," in touch with primal reality.

The other houses referred to in this parable of the
self may be identified with those wintry "white- and
high-roofed houses" of Jarrell's "Windows," in which
he dreamed of communion with the self of other hu-

THE LATER POEMS

man beings. If so, he refers to those houses here only in passing. Even the "houses" provided by the märchen that once were so fascinating to him are cold and dead. The only worlds that he now knows are the ones that he himself has made from the materials gathered on his solitary walks: the people, the animals, and the places he has known in the transitory days of his life.

A poem in *The Lost World* that concerns itself with the poet's making, and unmaking, of worlds is "Field and Forest." The speaker presents three images. The first is the general panorama of countryside one sees from an airplane, a monotonous patchwork of lines and colors signifying roads, tilled land, and forest. The second is the image of a farmer on that land, who appears close up, after the dark has leveled out the landscape and the farmer has undressed for bed, divesting himself of everything—clothes, glasses, movements of tongue and limb, and finally all the thoughts out of which he has made the world he lives in. Thus the reader has seen, at least in imagination, the wood-world of the previous poem and watched a solitary human being retreat from his re-creation of that world into his own House in the Wood. There in a third image, the farmer, reduced to a "blind wish," sees what he wants to see: a piece of his own lost world, created when, as a boy, he stood in the forest and stared at a fox in his den until he and the fox became one and for a brief moment occupied the center of a common universe.

This is what art enables us to do, Jarrell says in "The Old and the New Masters," a poem that begins by disagreeing with Auden's assertion in "Musée des Beaux Arts" that the old masters portrayed mankind generally as indifferent to human suffering. To show that Auden's generalization is too broad, Jarrell cites first La Tour's *St. Sebastian Mourned by St. Irene*, in which all eyes in the painting are fixed on the shaft that pierces the saint's chest, and then van der Goes' *Nativity*, in which the whole world seems to be concentrating on "this one instant" with the tiny babe "its small, helpless, human center." In describing both these paintings Jarrell calls into play the same discriminating intelligence that made his poems on Dürer's engraving and Donatello's *David* revelations for the student of works of art; but neither in the earlier poems nor here is Jarrell simply writing poems *about* art. As always he is looking beyond the work at hand to a revelation of his own, and here he makes that purpose explicit in twelve lines of added commentary. La Tour's Sebastian is a figure of Christ, and Sebastian's shaft, the spear that pierced Christ's side; van der Goes' figure at the center is Christ himself. But after these old masters, Jarrell goes on to say, new masters moved from symbol to realism and finally to abstract understanding, displacing not only Christ from the

THE LATER POEMS

center but earth itself. This is Jarrell on a private hobbyhorse, specifically his aversion to abstract art.[8] The counterweight for that aversion is his passion for the concrete, the solid data of day-to-day existence, which, however transitory, provide the only touch with reality we have or are likely to have.

The Lost World is full of such details, all transitory and all destined to be lost, but always treated with respect, even when they are clearly meant to be regarded as despicable. Jarrell's abiding love for things of this world is nowhere better expressed than in the thirteen-line poem entitled "Well Water," in which he compares the passing quanta of one's existence to clear, cold well water pumped from an old well, and by indirection he characterizes them as "the dailiness of life." Three poems in the book that are clearly recollections of Jarrell's "dailiness of life" may have seemed exotic to some of his readers. These are the poems about nocturnal flying creatures from his story for children *The Bat-Poet:* "The Mockingbird," "The Bird of Night" (an owl), and "Bats." These pieces fit neatly into the story of the little bat who had an irresistible impulse to write poetry; yet even when they are removed from their original context, as here, they speak eloquently to Jarrell's capacity for loving identification with nonhuman creatures—with the mockingbird who fought hard to make the world his own; with the owl whose fierce scrutiny reduced the night to stillness, much as the boy who stared at the fox briefly dominated the universe of those two; and with the bat mother who folds her wing about her sleeping children.

Other poems that also appear to have been taken directly from life are, on the whole, accessible to any careful reader and require little or no explanatory comment. "A Well-to-Do Invalid" is a monologue by an observer whose understanding grows as his sympathies shift from the invalid to the self-effacing wife who sacrificed her life to care for him. "The X-Ray Waiting Room in the Hospital" is the account by a patient, presumably Jarrell himself, of his enforced companionship with other smock-clad patients while he waits his turn to lie flat on a table for a myelogram, which turns out to be negative. "Three Bills" records a conversation overheard by Mary Jarrell at the Plaza Hotel in New York. Jarrell playfully turned the participants into hundred-thousand-dollar bills and made a poem of the incident that same afternoon.[9] Still another poem, "Washing," records and moralizes on a single afternoon's observation, this time a clothes line of washing flapping in a high breeze. Jarrell compares this to Michelangelo's depiction of his own flayed skin in *The Last Judgment* and then to a beheaded chicken running in circles in the yard. The washing seems to cry for help; but, Jarrell observes, the washing inhabits "a universe/ Indifferent to the woes of washing," and by implication indifferent to the woes of men and chickens as well. Finally, there is "In Galleries," a minor piece in which he contrasts the indifference (and possibly ignorance) of American museum guards with the genuine helpfulness of those in Italy.

More successful than any of these poems is "The One Who Was Different," a somewhat longer piece about the funeral of a woman whom Jarrell identifies only as Miss I——. The woman had been an eccentric in life, fond of cooking "straight through the cookbook," and like some educated spinsters of her generation given to wearing improbable combinations of dress and to taking cultural tours. But in death this inoffensive model of unorthodoxy has been subjected by her family to a series of enforced conformities, including a burial service with the customary words of St. Paul about putting on incorruption and immortality. The speaker is indignant. Possibly with a glance at Shakespeare's Barnadine in *Measure for Measure*, who had been drinking and declined to cooperate when they came to execute him, Jarrell chides himself for not having urged his friend simply to make up her mind to do without death and thus enjoy immortality without ever having to put it on. The point of this grimly playful poem, of course, is not a resentment against death, which would have been both sentimental and absurd on the face of it, but a serious affirmation of the need of the human spirit to resist the imposition of restrictive conventions and other empty formulas.

Something of the same attitude can be detected in "Hope," Jarrell's second poem of that title[10] and one of the longest poems in the canon. The speaker here is a man married to woman who is constitutionally disposed to exercise a motherly domination, and his hope is to escape to freedom. He returns with his wife to their fashionable apartment at two on Christmas morning and glances at the symbols of their fashionable taste, her taste actually—a harpsichord; paintings by Magnasco, Ensor, and Redon; a Norwegian grandfather's clock; a Kirman rug; pieces of collectible Americana scattered about; and a fir tree decorated with false snow and ice, standing on a hill of gifts. He recalls incidents from his childhood: the time when his mother's fainting spell briefly awoke in him the hope of escape; his father's ludicrous performances on Christmas morning, dispensing in the guise of Santa the gifts he had worked through the year to provide, then returning to the anonymity of his status of means to an end, an appendage to the kingdom of motherhood. His own house is filled with mothers, the speaker reflects—wife, cook, governess, maybe even the maid—and he grows irritable at the thought that his son is already showing symptoms of suffering the same kind of intimidation that has spoiled his own life. Nevertheless, he hopefully clings to the possibility that someday he may yet escape.

THE LATER POEMS

Another poem in *The Lost World* seems to objec-
tify the desire to escape from the domination of a father. This is the skillful narrative poem "A Hunt in the
Black Forest," published in an earlier form in *Poetry*,
1948, as "The King's Hunt".[11] The characters in the story
are a mute, whose tongue has been cut out presumably by order of the king (the mute has the brand of
the crown on his shoulder); his accomplice, a dwarf,
who lures the king to the mute's cottage in the woods;
and the hunter king, who helps himself to the mute's
stew and dies, poisoned, on the spot. Afterward the
mute peers in at the window to gaze on the dead king
crumpled over the table and, at the insistence of the
dwarf, holds him up to see. It is at this point that the
reader gets the suggestion of a meaning beneath the
surface of the story; for as the two faces peer in at the
window, they coalesce into a single face, that of a
child, something the reader has not seen before and
most likely never suspected. Yet this child, a combination of the two avenging personae, has clearly
planned and deftly executed the destruction of the
male authority figure oppressive to both halves of his
psyche. Ferguson calls attention to the fact that the
first two lines of this poem are almost identical with
the first two lines of "The Prince," a poem that first appeared in *The Seven-League Crutches*, three years
after the first version of the present poem. In both
poems these lines suggest the familiar situation of a
child's being put to bed in a darkened room and, from

the child's point of view, abandoned by the mother who has tucked him in and left, shutting the door behind her. Thus what the reader has here, is a fantasy or dream, fashioned after the material and pattern of fairy tales, in which a child, left to his own devices, confronts his darkest wishes and fears.

Five poems in Jarrell's last collection treat some aspect of the status of women in American society, a subject which intrigued and troubled him throughout his life. The first of these, placed at the beginning of the book, is called "Next Day"; it can be read as a later meditation by the woman at the Washington Zoo, assuming that that woman luckily found someone to "change" her and that she went on to become one of the sad hearts at the supermarket, old enough to command respect but no longer able to excite desire, old enough indeed to begin thinking at each funeral she attends that it might well have been her own. The poem catches a mood that is common to most people, however, men as well as women, as from time to time they are disaffected with "the dailiness of life" and wish they had somehow made themselves exceptional.

In "In Montecito" the point of view shifts to that of someone with superhuman powers of perception, and the poem presents the death of a woman, this time precisely identified (Greenie Taliaferro was her name), who was apparently more affluent than the unhappy woman in "Next Day." She was nonetheless

THE LATER POEMS

unhappy in her fashionable suburb, for the observer characterizes her as "a scream with breasts" and proceeds to describe what happened to that scream when lips, breasts, and all the other appendages that embodied it were stripped away. It hangs quite alone now in the night, the speaker says, while Greenie herself has gone on to join the transcendent suburb that surrounds Montecito like the echo of a scream. Although there is no sympathy for Greenie in this poem, the precisely designated suburbanite is probably incidental to the satiric intent of the poem. One notes that there is no sympathy here for Montecito either; and from that suburb of Santa Barbara, Jarrell's condemnation broadens out to include the whole range of American materialistic values.

Two poems in addition to "Next Day" are spoken by women and voice a contemporary woman's concerns. The first of these, "In Nature There Is Neither Right nor Left nor Wrong," is a slight, virtually self-explanatory piece in which a woman laments the whoredom she inadvertently contracted for when she consented to become a wife and mother. Dutifully, and not altogether unwillingly, she sleeps nightly with her fat, bald, rich husband but dreams of her first love, the serpent, who promised her something better than an automobile and fine gowns. In the second poem, "The Lost Children," the speaker joyfully accepts her role as mother and implicitly attributes any unhappiness she may experience in it to the nature of things. As other commentators have noted, this poem, one of Jarrell's most appealing, was made up out of an account of a dream that Mary Jarrell wrote down at her husband's suggestion, and some of the language in the poem is hers.[12] The children in the poem are the daughters of the speaker. Both are lost, one through death at an early age, the other simply through growing up and away from her mother's care. The poem proceeds in a series of irregular unrhymed units that function as stanzas—the technique that Jarrell used most often in his later work—to set forth the maturation of the living child. At first she is an unborn fetus, then a suckling infant, and after that a child capable of having adventures on her own. In all these stages, even though progressively independent, she still belongs to the parent; but at last she reaches a point where she deliberately distances herself from her mother. At that point she takes permanent leave, perhaps writing once a week or, after a time, bringing home a husband to look at the old photograph albums with her. Nevertheless, the mother keeps in one corner of her mind her offspring, both dead and living, as ageless children, and they reappear to her from time to time in her happiest dreams. The one who died looks at her briefly and disappears, but the other tirelessly plays hide-and-seek with her, staying in sight usually, but always just out of reach.

THE LATER POEMS

The last poem in this group, "Woman," extends the range to include other roles that a woman may perform in the world that Jarrell envisions for her. Ferguson, a sympathetic critic, has characterized the poem as "a funny, grudging panegyric to Everywoman."[13] It is certainly all this, and more. The speaker, whom readers will have difficulty in not identifying with Jarrell, clearly adores the woman who has taken the place of a mother in his life and states his adoration in terms that can only be called extravagant. Yet this paragon among women is also child, guardian, wife, mistress, student, teacher, both Diana and Venus; and the resulting contradictions in his image of her compel him to qualify his praise with an admixture of satire which, as Beck has put it, "might not delight the heart of a feminist."[14] Perhaps equally disturbing to some is the speaker's assumption that this wonderful creature exists primarily as a complement to his life as a male. She is totally committed to her mate and seems to neither have nor seek any kind of independent existence. Most disturbing of all to the critic, however, is the suspicion that this poem is a piece primarily confessional and rhetorical. The alternation of praise and witty undercutting, though amusing, does not permit the emergence of a credible image and thus does not entirely satisfy. For many of his readers, as perhaps it did for Jarrell himself, the enigma that he presents in this woman remains intact.

The enigma of woman is intact also in the two major poems that give the book its title: "The Lost World" and "Thinking of the Lost World." In the first of these frankly autobiographical pieces Jarrell re-creates in a three-part poem his memorable twelfth year spent with his paternal grandparents (Mama and Pop) and great-grandmother (Dandeen) in the Los Angeles of 1925–26. At that time Los Angeles was a relatively small city, made glamorous and famous by the presence of the movie industry; and the memories of that early Los Angeles that Jarrell records in the poem include a cameraman perched on a platform on the bumper of a car, the Metro-Goldwyn-Mayer lion, which he visited, and, as noted earlier, the papier-mâché figures of pterodactyl and dinosaur on Melrose Avenue, properties for the filming of Conan Doyle's *The Lost World.* The form of the poem—a series of fairly regular iambic lines in terza rima—"nods at Dante," says Ferguson; but Jarrell's nod here is probably more immediately directed at Allen Tate, who used the form in "The Swimmers" and "The Buried Lake," the two published parts of his own long auto-biographical poem.[15] Except for the rhyme scheme Jarrell's "Lost World" has nothing in common with Dante's poem.

The first section, subtitled "Children's Arms," focuses on the boy's "real world," a platform in a euca-lyptus tree, and the arms by which he defends it: a

THE LATER POEMS

copper helmet and breastplace that Pop, a metal worker, has made for him, a shield of beaver board, a bow with eleven arrows, a knife, and an unpainted wooden biplane. This is his own little state, his Rome, in which the pet rabbit, Reddy, is his only dependent. In territories round about, the boy enters temporarily a succession of communities that are only somewhat less real: he watches a senior play (this year it's Barrie's *The Admirable Crichton*); he makes a Saturday visit to Pop's dimly lighted workshop (this reminds him of the cave of the Niebelungs); and, with Mama's permission, he rides to the local library with Mrs. Mercer in her gray electric. Briefer impressions provide data that extend and enrich this remembered world: the half dog, half wolf that sits beside him on the back seat of Mrs. Mercer's car, the bud vases with yellow roses by the back window, the sound of a Chopin prelude from next door, and his dream of a mysterious tall girl, from which his grandmother wakes him at the beginning of his Saturday holiday.

In part 2, "A Night with Lions," he recalls visiting "my aunt's friend / Who owned a lion." The aunt ("young, tall, brown") seems to be the tall girl of his dream in the preceding section, and she, not the Metro-Goldwyn-Mayer lion (who is also the lion of *Tarzan*), is the dominant figure in this one. Lying down to sleep that night, after dutifully putting the lion in his prayer, the boy fancies that he is lying beside her, almost breathless at the sound of her voice and sight of her skin but engaging in serious conversation about such mature subjects as *Jurgen* and Rupert Hughes.

Part 3, "A Street off Sunset" (Sunset Boulevard), begins with an explicit avowal of the retrospective nature of the whole poem. Randall Jarrell, now a resident not of a street off Sunset but of Greensboro, North Carolina, observes, as he was in the habit of doing to friends and colleagues, that the pungent odor emanating from the Vick Chemical Company calls to mind his eucalyptus tree in Los Angeles. He goes on to say that after rubbing his chest with the ointment, he can dispense with his intervening lifetime and sit once more in the blue sedan beside Dandeen as they ride along the Boulevard with its succession of garish signs and buildings. After they have returned to the street off Sunset, he arranges himself crossways in an armchair and begins to read a piece in *Amazing Stories* about a mad scientist who planned to destroy the world. From this point on, the man's recollection proceeds in an orderly fashion through a period of twenty-four hours. First he goes to bed, presumably to sleep, though actually he puts on earphones and drifts off gradually as he listens to Aimee Semple McPherson proclaim the Four-Square Gospel. Then suddenly it is morning again and time for the daily routines of breakfast and school. In the afternoon he plays dominoes with Dandeen and listens more or less patiently

THE LATER POEMS

to her stories of the War Between the States. At last he manages to break away to feed his rabbit. No sooner has he reached the yard, however, than his grandmother comes out to kill a chicken; and the boy, seeing the death of the bird and the momentary insensitivity of the adult who has accomplished it, fears for his rabbit and will not be entirely consoled. Yet he wants very much to trust his grandmother; and trying hard to ignore the shock of seeing her with a chicken's head in her hand, he returns quickly but uneasily to his almost equally troubling magazine story. The poem ends with Pop's return from work; and we last see the two of them, boy and grandfather, sitting on the steps in the sunset at the end of their "good day," the grandfather assuring him that mad scientists are only make-believe.

"Thinking of the Lost World" is a companion piece to the foregoing, but it comes last in the volume. The poem begins with a Proustlike observation that the spoonful of chocolate tapioca pudding he has just put into his mouth tastes like the vanilla extract that Mama once told him not to drink. Now, however, the mature Jarrell is sitting in Greensboro with his wife, recalling a recent trip to California, where they looked for vestiges of the lost childhood but found the California sun turned to gray and all the familiar places, people, and things vanished. Jarrell wishes he could find the blue sedan and the gray electric in some museum of old cars, and maybe a crystal set that would let him tune in to the voices he heard as a child, especially that of the tall brown aunt, who first awoke sexual stirrings within him and since then has returned repeatedly in many guises. He never saw her again, never wrote to her; but, he tells himself reassuringly, nothing is ever absolutely gone. Nothing of his lost world need be dead as long as he is there to recover it: the chicken going round in circles, the mad scientist, Mama and Pop and Dandeen.

He thinks of the young people he knows now, perhaps his Greensboro students, who can't tell the first World War from the second; thinks of the smaller children who see his graying beard and call him Santa Claus; and looks at the hand on the wheel of his car, already brown and spotted like Mama's. But he also sees before him the image of a boy in tennis shoes and khaki riding-pants and reaches out his hand. It comes back empty. Clearly the lost world is not something he can hold in his hands; yet he does hold it in memory, where re-created in dream or in poetry it can be a possession and a happiness forever, something never again to be lost.

Everyone, of course, has his or her own version of the lost world, and many take at least a degree of pleasure in recalling it. It is not altogether surprising, therefore, that some early reviewers of Jarrell's last book were irritated that he should presume to impose the undisguised particulars of a private lost world on the general reading public; but Jarrell had a variety of precedents in both verse and prose—among them Wordsworth, Rilke, Kipling, and Proust—and he knew what he was doing. Others knew too and praised *The Lost World* for its masterful use of natural speech rhythms, its subtle development of themes and subjects that had preoccupied him for two decades, its broad humanity, and its masterful treatment of childhood, without triteness and without sentimentality. Those who knew Jarrell best saw that in openly recovering his past and integrating it with the verifiable data of the present, he was simply doing publicly what he had always done in his best writing: making it an adjunct to reality as he had been given to perceive reality, with his senses, in his dreams, and in his waking memory. *The Lost World Recovered* would have been an immodest title for his last book, but it would have described accurately the nature of his accomplishment there and suggested the maturity of talent that had enabled him to achieve it. There was clearly more to come.

Jarrell would probably have been pleased with *The Complete Poems*, which in 1969, four years after his death, reprinted without change *Selected Poems*, *The Woman at the Washington Zoo*, and *The Lost World*. For the benefit of the growing number of serious students of Jarrell's work, that volume brought back into print those poems from "The Rage for the

Lost Penny" (1940) and the four earlier books that Jarrell had omitted when he put together *Selected Poems*, along with forty-one published poems that he had never put into a collection and forty-five unpublished ones in varying states of completion. Jarrell was a good critic of his own work; he had already decided against printing most of this material, and probably would not have changed his mind about that. The seven new pieces in *The Complete Poems* are quite another matter. Most of these very likely would have gone into the volume *Let's See*, which Jarrell was planning at the time of his death, and they constitute the one clear indication extant of the direction his poetry was taking.[16]

One of the seven was "The Owl's Bedtime Story," in terza rima, which was subsequently published as a part of the children's story *Fly By Night*. Another was a translation of Rilke's "Das Lied des Blinden." "Gleaning" is a brief monologue by a poor black woman, grown old, who recalls, with side glances at the story of Ruth in the Bible, a lifetime of gleaning in California bean fields and her experiences with men there. "Say Good-bye to Big Daddy" is an elegy on Big Daddy Lipscomb, the star player for the Baltimore Colts, who died of an overdose of heroin. The poem looks at the black player's formidable size, the magnanimity on the field that distinguished him, and the fears that haunted him; it ends with the ironic and characteristically Jarrellian comment that world will not—and,

THE LATER POEMS

alas, will—be the same without Big Daddy. These poems are very much worth having; but the remaining three, all in the unrhymed iambics of Jarrell's latest work and all built out of the hard particulars of his immediate life, are even more interesting.

"The Augsburg Adoration" is not another "poem about art," though it mentions art and artists, but a reflection about the permanence effected by natural recurrence in a world of change. The data of the poem come from the trip that the Jarrells made to Europe in 1963, specifically from visits to Augsburg, Ulm, and perhaps Rome, though the last may have been remembered from an earlier visit. In all these places the speaker is confronted by mankind's symbols of permanence—sculpture in stone, cathedral spire, Roman monuments—all destined to decay; yet at all of them he has seen the same sparrows, who differ in no way from the sparrows who cheeped to Mozart, Goethe, and the Duke of Wellington or from those who brought food to their young in Jesus' Nazareth. Again one sees that nature, by incorporating change, achieves a degree of permanence that art alone can never achieve.

"The Player Piano" appears to have resulted from a summer visit to Blowing Rock, North Carolina, where the Pancake House, locally owned and operated, was a popular spot. There the speaker (we learn only near the end of the poem that the speaker is a woman) discovers that the woman running the place is from

California, and that discovery leads to an exchange of recollections, which in turn precipitates even further recollections when the speaker returns to her hotel. Looking at a photograph of her parents, from whom she has long been emotionally alienated, she realizes the family difficulties for which she has always blamed them were really the mistakes of very young people not absolutely responsible for the pain that had resulted from their actions. The point of the poem comes into focus as the speaker sees herself as a child holding her hands above the keys of their player piano and "playing at playing" the instrument, which performs its Chopin waltz in obedience to an authority the child cannot see or know.[17]

Perhaps the most interesting poem in this group is "A Man Meets a Woman in the Street," which Mary Jarrell had printed as a part of her essay in *Randall Jarrell 1914-1965*. Like "Woman" of *The Lost World* it celebrates the relationship between a man passing middle age and his somewhat younger wife, but it does so in a credible dramatic situation, and it recognizes realities in the situation and avoids extravagances that the earlier poem slipped into. The situation is a simple one. The man sees his wife walking ahead of him on a New York street, fancifully plays with the notion that she is a stranger he would like to meet, then catches up with her and rejoices that she is all the things he had ever wished for in a woman.

THE LATER POEMS

He recalls that before he began his latest trip to the city, he had been accustomed to wishing, as men normally wish, that the day at hand might be different. Now suddenly he understands the need to wish as birds do, and his only wish, at this moment of a simple and inconsequential gesture, is that nothing will change. In short, his wish and his life are now the same thing; and with that slightly puzzling affirmation we get a hint of the new level of awareness that Jarrell was beginning to explore at the time of his death.

At first reading one might say that this poem comes dangerously close to sentimentality and that, moreover, the wish to avoid change contradicts Jarrell's repeated insistence in previous poems that the price of life is pain and change. The phrase "birds' wish" should prevent such conclusions. It should at least call to mind his account of the sparrows at Augsburg, Ulm, and Rome and their transcendence of change by accepting it. For these creatures, as for all of Jarrell's nonhuman characters, wishes, as human beings understand wishes, are by their very nature frivolous. For birds, rabbits, dogs, cats, and bats, wishing and being are the same; and it is the "natural wisdom" of these creatures that the man exuberantly in love with his wife achieves briefly on the Manhattan street. Like them he accepts his "good day" as the child does at the end of "The Lost World" and wishes for nothing beyond the happiness of being as he is. The poem acknowledges fully the pain and change that have brought these two people to this point, and it nowhere suggests that their joy of the moment can be prolonged. It simply joins centuries of great poetry in affirming that happiness and beauty, however evanescent in the passage of time, can be joys forever.

Notes

1. Suzanne Ferguson, *The Poetry of Randall Jarrell* (Baton Rouge: Louisiana State University Press, 1971) 156–57.

2. Jarrell's account of how he wrote this poem, originally prepared for the third edition of Brooks and Warren's *Understanding Poetry*, appears in *A Sad Heart at the Supermarket* (New York: Atheneum, 1962) 160–73.

3. Ferguson 159.

4. Commentary on this poem is available in Charlotte H. Beck, *World and Lives: The Poetry of Randall Jarrell* (Port Washington, NY: Associated Faculty Press, 1983) 86–89; in Ferguson 162–67; and in Bernetta Quinn, "Jarrell's Desert of the Heart," *Analects* 1 (1961): 25–26.

5. Ferguson 156.

6. An essay on Jarrell as translator, especially of Rilke, is Ingo Seidler's "Jarrell and the Art of Translation," *Analects* 1 (1961): 37–48. See also Richard K. Cross, "Jarrell's Translations: The Poet as Elective Middle European," *Critical Essays on Randall Jarrell,* ed. Suzanne Ferguson (Boston: G. K. Hall, 1983) 310–20.

7. *Randall Jarrell, 1914–1965,* ed. Robert Lowell, Peter Taylor, and Robert Penn Warren (New York: Farrar, Straus, 1967) contains among its collection of photographs (at p. 164) one of this figure.

8. See his essay "Against Abstract Expressionism," *Kipling, Auden & Co.* (New York: Farrar, Straus, 1980) 285–89.

THE LATER POEMS

9. See the commentary by Ferguson, *Poetry of Randall Jarrell* 192–93 and Beck, 63–66.

10. See *The Complete Poems* (New York: Farrar, Straus, 1969) 111.

11. See Ferguson, *Poetry of Randall Jarrell* 198.

12. See Beck, 43–44 and Ferguson, *Poetry of Randall Jarrell* 209–12.

13. Ferguson, *Poetry of Randall Jarrell* 203.

14. Beck, 18.

15. Like most of the poems of *The Lost World,* this tripartite poem presents few obstacles to the reader. Ferguson, *Poetry of Randall Jarrell* 212–20, has the fullest account of it.

16. See Mary Jarrell, "The Group of Two," *Randall Jarrell, 1914–1965* 298.

17. Mary Jarrell writes that her husband "wrote 'The Player Piano' and forgave his parents everything," *Randall Jarrell, 1914–1965* 296.

BIBLIOGRAPHY

Works by Randall Jarrell

Poetry, Essays, and Fiction

"The Rage for the Lost Penny." *Five Young American Poets.* Norfolk, CT: New Directions, 1940. 81–123. Jarrell's first collection of poems in book form; his contribution includes a brief introduction.

Blood for a Stranger. New York: Harcourt, Brace, 1942. Poetry.

Little Friend, Little Friend. New York: Dial, 1945. Poetry.

Losses. New York: Harcourt, Brace, 1948. Poetry.

The Seven-League Crutches. New York: Harcourt, Brace, 1951. Poetry.

Poetry and the Age. New York: Knopf, 1953; London: Faber & Faber, 1955. Essays.

Pictures from an Institution. New York: Knopf, 1954; London: Faber & Faber, 1954. Novel.

Selected Poems. New York: Knopf, 1955; London: Faber & Faber, 1956. Poetry.

The Woman at the Washington Zoo. New York: Atheneum, 1960. Poetry.

A Sad Heart at the Supermarket. New York: Atheneum, 1962; London: Eyre & Spottiswoode, 1965. Essays.

The Gingerbread Rabbit. New York: Macmillan, 1964; London: Collier-Macmillan, 1964. Children's story.

The Bat-Poet. New York: Macmillan, 1964; London: Collier-Macmillan, 1964. Children's story / poetry.

The Lost World. New York: Macmillan, 1965; London: Collier-Macmillan, 1965. Poetry.

The Animal Family. New York: Pantheon, 1965; London: Hart-Davis, 1967. Children's story.

BIBLIOGRAPHY

The Complete Poems. New York: Farrar, Straus, 1969; London: Faber & Faber, 1971.

The Third Book of Criticism. New York: Farrar, Straus, 1969; London: Faber & Faber, 1975. Essays.

Fly by Night. New York: Farrar, Straus, 1976; London: Bodley Head, 1977. Children's story / poetry.

Kipling, Auden & Co.: Essays and Reviews 1935-1964. New York: Farrar, Straus, 1980; London: Carcanet, 1981.

Randall Jarrell's Letters. An Autobiographical and Literary Selection. Ed. Mary Jarrell. Boston: Houghton Mifflin, 1985. Biographical commentary interspersed.

Translations

The Golden Bird, and Other Fairy Tales of the Brothers Grimm. New York: Macmillan, 1962.

The Rabbit Catcher and Other Fairy Tales of Ludwig Bechstein. New York: Macmillan, 1962.

Anton Chekhov: The Three Sisters. New York: Macmillan, 1969.

Snow-White and the Seven Dwarfs: A Tale from the Brothers Grimm. New York: Farrar, Straus, 1972.

Goethe's Faust: Part I. New York: Farrar, Straus, 1976.

Edited Books

The Anchor Book of Stories. Garden City, NY: Doubleday Anchor, 1958.

The Best Short Stories of Rudyard Kipling. Garden City, NY: Hanover House, 1961.

The English in England: Short Stories by Rudyard Kipling. Garden City, NY: Doubleday Anchor, 1963.

In the Vernacular: The English in India. Garden City, NY: Doubleday Anchor, 1963.

Six Russian Short Novels. Garden City, NY: Doubleday Anchor, 1963.

BIBLIOGRAPHY

Selected Works about Randall Jarrell

Bibliographies / Checklists

Adams, Charles. *Randall Jarrell: A Bibliography.* Chapel Hill: University of North Carolina Press, 1958. Supplement in *Analects* 1 (S, 1961): 49–56.

Gilliken, Dure J. "A Check-List of Criticism on Randall Jarrell, 1941–1970, with an introduction and a List of his Major Works." *Bulletin of the New York Public Library* 74 (Apr. 1971): 176–94.

Kisslinger, Margaret V. "A Bibliography of Randall Jarrell, 1958–1965." *Bulletin of Bibliography* 24 (May–Aug. 1966): 243–47.

Shapiro, Karl. *Randall Jarrell.* Washington, DC: Library of Congress, 1967. Pamphlet. Contains a 1966 memorial lecture, presented under the auspices of the Gertrude Clarke Whittall Poetry and Literature Fund, and a bibliography of Jarrell materials in the Library of Congress.

Wright, Stuart. *Randall Jarrell: A Descriptive Bibliography, 1929–1983.* Charlottesville, VA: Bibliographical Society of the University of Virginia, 1986.

Books

Beck, Charlotte H. *World and Lives: The Poetry of Randall Jarrell.* Port Washington, NY: Associated Faculty Press, 1983. Criticism of the poetry, concentrating on monologues, dialogues, and narrative scenes.

Ferguson, Suzanne. *The Poetry of Randall Jarrell.* Baton Rouge: Louisiana State University Press, 1971. A comprehensive critical study of the poetry.

_____, ed. *Critical Essays on Randall Jarrell.* Boston: G. K. Hall, 1983. Contains, in the introduction, a good survey of critical and scholarly studies; selected reviews; essays by M. Bernetta

BIBLIOGRAPHY

Quinn, Jerome Mazzaro, Helen Hagenbüchle, William H. Pritchard, Parker Tyler, Richard Fein, Frances Ferguson, Russell Fowler, Charlotte Beck, Mary Kinzie, Leven Dawson, David Cornelius, Michel Benamou, Janet Sharistanian, Keith Monroe, Sylvia Angus, Suzanne Ferguson, Kathe Davis Finney, Ingo Seidler, and Richard K. Cross.

Hoffman, Frederic J. *The Achievement of Randall Jarrell. A Comprehensive Selection of His Poems with a Critical Introduction.* Glenview, IL: Scott, Foresman, 1970.

Lowell, Robert, Peter Taylor, and Robert Penn Warren, eds. *Randall Jarrell, 1914–1965.* New York: Farrar, Straus, 1967. Essays by Hannah Arendt, John Berryman, Elizabeth Bishop, Philip Booth, Cleanth Brooks, James Dickey, Denis Donoghue, Leslie A. Fiedler, Robert Fitzgerald, R. W. Flint, Alfred Kazin, Stanley Kunitz, Robert Lowell, William Meredith, Marianne Moore, Robert Phelps, M. Bernetta Quinn, John Crowe Randson, Adrienne Rich, Delmore Schwartz, Maurice Sendak, Karl Shapiro, Allen Tate, Eleanor Ross Taylor, P. L. Travers, Robert Watson, Mary Jarrell.

Quinn, M. Bernetta. *Randall Jarrell.* Boston: Twayne, 1981. A survey of Jarrell's work, with emphasis on the poetry; biographical material interspersed.

Rosenthal, M. L. *Randall Jarrell.* University of Minnesota Pamphlets on American Writers No. 103. Minneapolis: University of Minnesota Press, 1972. An introductory survey.

Articles and Parts of Books

Beck, Charlotte H. "Randall Jarrell's Modernism: The Sweet Uses of Personae." *South Atlantic Quarterly* 50 (1985): 67–75. Jarrell's use of dramatic and confessional strategies in his monologues.

Bedient, Calvin. "The Critics Who Made Us: Randall Jarrell and *Poetry and the Age*." *Sewanee Review* 93 (W, 1985): 128–35.

BIBLIOGRAPHY

Concentrates on the one volume but gives a general evaluation of Jarrell as critic.

Ciardi, John, ed. *Mid-Century American Poets.* Boston: Twayne, 1950. 182–201. Jarrell's answers to twelve questions about his work, followed by a selection of poems.

Humphrey, Robert. "Randall Jarrell's Poetry." *Themes and Directions in American Literature: Essays in Honor of Leon Howard,* eds. Ray B. Browne and Donald B. Pizer. Lafayette, IN: Purdue University Press, 1972. 220–32. The dependence of Jarrell's poetry on psychoanalytic theory, and its relation to the work of Frost and Rilke.

Mazzaro, Jerome. *Postmodern American Poetry.* Champaign: University of Illinois Press, 1980. 32–58. Evaluation of the poetry as an only partially successful resolution of contradictions in the poet himself but a significant attempt to apply psychological techniques to American themes.

Nemerov, Howard. "Randall Jarrell: A Myth About Poetry." *Reflexions on Poetry and Politics.* New Brunswick, NJ: Rutgers University Press, 1972. 96–99. Review of *The Complete Poems* with comments on the myth that grows, in language, out of the details of a poet's life.

Pratt, William. "Jarrell as Critic." *The Mississippi Quarterly* 34 (F, 1981): 477–84. Focuses on *Kipling, Auden & Co.* but gives a general evaluation of Jarrell as critic.

Quinn, M. Bernetta. "Jarrell's Desert of the Heart." *Analects* 1. (S, 1961): 24–28. The theme of isolation in Jarrell's poetry.

———. *The Metamorphic Tradition in Modern Poetry.* 2nd ed. New York: Gordian Press, 1966. 168–206. The theme of metamorphosis in Jarrell's early poetry.

———. *Randall Jarrell.* Contemporary Authors Bibliographical Series 2. ed. Ronald Baughman. Detroit: Gale Research Company, 1986.

BIBLIOGRAPHY

Ramsay, Paul. "In Exasperation and Gratitude." *Sewanee Review* 74 (1966): 930–45. Contains a review of *Selected Poems* with useful comments on "The Märchen."

Rideout, Walter B. "To Change! to Change." *Poets in Progress,* ed. Edward Hungerford. Evanston, IL: Northwestern University Press, 1967. 156–78. Reviews Jarrell's achievement in poetry through *The Woman at the Washington Zoo.*

Seidler, Ingo. "Jarrell and the Art of Translation." *Analects* 1 (S, 1961): 37–48. Deals with translations, principally Rilke, published through 1961.

Taylor, Peter. "That Cloistered Jazz." *Michigan Quarterly Review* 5 (F, 1966): 237–45. The writer as teacher, with reminiscences about Jarrell at Kenyon and the University of North Carolina at Greensboro.

INDEX

INDEX

INDEX

INDEX

INDEX

INDEX

INDEX

INDEX

INDEX